Café
DESIGN
NUMBER TWO

Café
DESIGN

NUMBER TWO

MARTIN M. PEGLER

Visual Reference Publications, Inc. ▪ New York

Visual Reference Publications
302 Fifth Avenue
New York, NY 10001

Distributors to the trade in the United States and Canada
Watson-Guptill Publishers
1515 Broadway
New York, NY 10036

Distributors outside the United Sates and Canada
HarperCollins International
10 E. 53rd Street
New York, NY 10022

Library of Congress Cataloging in Publication Data:
Café Design
Printed in Hong Kong
ISBN 1058471-074-8
Designed by Dutton & Sherman

CONTENTS

INTRODUCTION

This edition of Café Design has been assembled and accessorized as carefully and thoughtfully as a bridal ensemble for that auspicious day. From around the world—quite literally—we have found "something old" (in this case "traditional"), "something new" (the latest in technologies and materials), "something borrowed" (a tribute to the many ethnic cuisines now popular in cafés and bistros) and even "something blues" (since music—more and more—is part of the dining experience). We have also "traveled" north to Canada to find the Italian-inspired Basilico and as far south as Brazil where the Japanese community and the Brazilians as a whole can enjoy the ethnic foods served in Kosushi. If east is near east—there is Frangipani in Mumbai, India where Asian/fusion food is all the rage and if California can be considered the west, then there are numerous choices as well. What's new in dining pleasures in Las Vegas? It's here! Where do the Romans go when they want a taste of the USA? We have that—and we have numerous projects that show where and how the Taste of Italy is expressed across the USA; from glorified pizzerias to upper echelon, gourmet Tuscan cookery. Want fun, flash, color, pizzazz and all that jazz? You'll find cafés and bistros where all the above reign. And—you haven't seen anything yet!

The criteria for selecting the projects you'll find in this book is quite simple: casual, relaxed, fun, colorful—a place where a man might wear as jacket but a tie is just an add-on. A place where even if the table-cloth and napkins are starchy and white—the ambiance is not. A place where a diner might fall in love at first sight and never tire of going back again and again—and that's before even tasting the food. No matter how elegant and epicurean the cuisine may be, the ambiance does affect the taste of the food. Quality and quantity are important, but today—even more so—comfort is too. People eat out not because they need sustenance, they dine out for a pleasurable experience that not only fills them up gastronomically but captures and involves all of their senses: from the sounds that surround them—the colors and lights—the aromas and perfumes of foods and flowers—to the feel of the floor beneath their feet—the covers on the banquettes and benches, the china and crystal. They are all part of the dining experience and they all count.

To facilitate your gastronomic tour through Café Design No. 2, the projects are loosely grouped by cuisine. By flipping through the Italian, French and Asian menu-inspired cafés/bistros/trattoria/noodle houses/sushi bars, etc., the viewer can see the vast variations that can be developed on a theme depending upon location, space and the targeted diner. There is also a cluster of traditional steak houses and grills with relaxed bars and cafés as well as music-oriented venues.

As always, may you enjoy this visual, virtual voyage and I hope all your senses are stimulated by what you see—especially your sense of inspiration.

Martin M. Pegler

Café

DESIGN

NUMBER TWO

GIORDANO'S

CHICAGO, IL

Design ▪ Lieber Cooper Associates, Chicago, IL

Design Team ▪ Marve Cooper/Keith Curtis/Lisa Simeone/Starr Percel

Photographer ▪ Mark Ballogg, Steinkamp Ballogg, Chicago, IL

A visitor to Chicago may get to stroll the Million Dollar Mile, see the Sears and Hancock towers high over the skyline, be battered and be ill-treated by the city's notoriously changeable weather but they really haven't tasted the real "Chicago" until they have dug in and savored one of Giordano's "Chicago stuffed pizzas." This "must" has been a Chicago landmark and tradition for over a

quarter of a century and this delicacy can now be sampled in any of the 35 Giordano's located throughout the greater Chicago area.

Lieber Cooper Associates of Chicago accepted the challenge presented to them and shown here is the new/old look for Giordano's: warm, traditional, and "a local environment using humble materials." Taking its lead from the client, LCA maintained the company's signature logo "to accentuate its Chicago roots and neighborhood pizzeria quality" as well as create a brand identity for the chain both in the city and in the suburbs. "The artistic decoration employs familiar artifacts capturing Chicago's blues and jazz music and satirical humor."

Comfortable booths upholstered in bold stripes of black, red and viridian vinyl, separated by dark wood dividers, are set along side the ocher gold walls which are laden with framed posters, newspaper pages and myriad old-time photographs. Up front, in the entrance and bar area, the floor is laid with miniature hexagonal-shaped black and white ceramic tiles in patterns and borders while a mostly red, boldly patterned carpet takes over in the rear dining area. In the dining zone red velvet drapery contrasts with the dark stained wood paneled walls and the florid design on the banquette that runs beneath the picture-encrusted back wall. The red vinyl chairs are

complemented by the signature red and white checkered tablecloths with crisp white toppers. To one side of the room is a low mezzanine with dark stained wood flooring and a combination of loose and booth seating. Old fashioned ribbed crystal lighting fixtures hang down over the dining area and accentuate the red and gold of the setting. A semi brick wall only partially screens off the active kitchen with pizza oven and gleaming, copper trimmed venting hoods. The back wall, over the open kitchen, has the feeling of an old, weather-worn and exposed brick wall with remnants of painted signage on it.

This prototype design will be used as Giordano's rolls out even more pizzerias that "communicate a message that Giordano's is a friendly, heartland restaurant for everyone."

TONY & BRUNO'S

MERRICK, NY

Design ▪ Morris Nathanson Design, Pawtucket, RI
Photography ▪ Warren Jagger Photography,
Providence, RI

Sbarro is a name well known on the East Coast of the country as a pizzeria/fast food Italian-style chain of outlets in highly visible locations. To add to their list of holdings, Sbarro's requested that Morris Nathanson Design of Pawtucket create a new look for the Tony & Bruno's operation. The client's brief was "to create a casual café/restaurant that would include major takeout abilities and also offer a casual dining experience."

The 3500 sq. ft. floor plan is divided into two distinct areas. The forward area boasts a 25 ft. long impressive pizza line featuring a brick oven. The other area is the more "formal" dining room. "All the

materials selected were considered for their ability to provide this scene of authenticity but also for concerns of maintenance." Thus, the designers specified popular priced furniture, light fixtures and tile work—all to establish the desired casual dining setting. Medium stained wood floors, sponge painted walls in wholesome and hearty yellow ochers and the wood grained lower partitions all add to the desired ambiance. Traditional red and white checkered cloths under white paper square toppers complement the tawny gold upholstery on the dark wood chairs and banquettes while the booths are upholstered in black vinyl. Wood frames with frosted glass panels provide a modicum of privacy for those in the booths lined up under the picture and poster layered walls. Because of the client's "authentically and long standing background for serving Italian American food," Josh Nathanson, the lead designer on this project, included many framed photographs that feature historical scenes of Italian American neighborhood culture. To many of the locals of Merrick, NY—a suburb of New York City—this is all new, but to the older residents who originally came from the old time Italian neighborhoods in Brooklyn, Manhattan and the Bronx—it is like coming home.

To welcome the "old timers" home and make the younger patrons feel more comfortable, the exterior design "attempts to present the classic elements associated with neighborhood cafés." Brightly-striped canvas awnings, the "tomato-sauce label" style signage and the glowing lights do it. So does the view of the pizza line, the brick oven, and the boldly patterned red and yellow checkerboard tiled back wall—all seen through the many tall windows set in the warm brick facade.

JOEY D'ATTORE'S

CHARLOTTE, NC

Design ▪ Little & Associates, Architects, Atlanta, GA
Photography ▪ Prakash Patel Photography

A visit to Joey D'Attore's—or as familiarly known, Joey D's—in a shopping mall just outside of Charlotte, NC is like taking a step back to another time and place. As conceived and designed by Little & Associates, Architects of Atlanta, GA, the 6400 sq. ft. Italian restaurant is more than a little reminiscent of what we think a neighborhood spaghetti house would look like in 1940 Brooklyn, Little Italy or Hoboken. To make that bygone era come to life, a fictional character—Joey D—has been created and this warm, down-to-earth and solid setting is his place. Friends and family are invited to enjoy the homey quality of the food as though Grandma were out in the kitchen stirring the pots and adding a little more garlic to the sauce.

The walnut floors and deep mahogany stained chairs, tables and millwork create a feeling of "old times" while the burgundy carpeting in the dining room, the dark red vinyl material used to upholster the tufted, curved booths and the recurring red and white checkered cloths all add to the warmth of the space. Walls and the upper parts of the Corinthian columns are painted a healthy cream color and the walls are filled with dozens of nostalgic family pic-

tures (mostly in black and white) and in simple dark frames. The 40's era is recalled in the art moderne sweeping mahogany and stainless partitions that encircle the dining area and the inverted pyramid shaped light fixtures set into recessed openings in the ceiling that are highlighted by the borders of deep burgundy color. The same color is used around the lower parts of the columns that are stationed across the enclosed seating area. The small black and white, hexagonal ceramic tiles used around the bar and the columns to either side of the curved, granite topped bar recall an even earlier time; a saloon at the turn of the century—the 19th into the 20th. The

mulberry/burgundy color also accentuates the 14 ft., ceiling high wine rack that is the focal element in the bar area. Glass shelves cross over the large window that is incorporated into the back bar and more liquor is displayed here. The bar is separated from the seating by a vaulted ceiling.

Through the 14 ft. high windows a visual connection is made with the outdoor courtyard where more diners can be seated. Red Mountain Management, the parent company of Joey D'Attore's, targeted this operation towards the middle and upper income suburban couples and families—and they appear to have hit their mark.

ANTICO POSTO

OAK BROOK, IL

Design ▪ Aria Group Architects, Oak Park, IL
Photography ▪ Mark Ballogg, Steinkamp/
Ballogg, Chicago, IL

It is "look backwards in time" time. Enter Antico Posto—The Old Spot—and it is like entering a time warp and suddenly there are no computers, cell phones, and palm pilots and people have time to sit back, relax, be friendly and enjoy old-time, old-fashioned "home made," family style food.

As conceived and designed by the Aria Group of Oak Park, IL for the always fun, adventurous and fin-ger-on-the-public's pulse, successful Lettuce Entertain You Enterprises, this Italian trattoria could be anyplace but in upscale Oak Park. Maybe—and more likely—in downtown Chicago in the 1920s and 1930s. Adding to the ambiance are the natural wood floors and wain-scoting, the simple wood divider that cuts across the space to create a long banquette on either side of it and more intimate booths on the other side while taking full advantage of the structural column that stands center in the space. Other "warming" touches are the rich, ocher gold faux painted walls and upper columns. The charcoal brown painted ceiling "disappears" but the eye is attracted to the glazed white ceramic band, framed in dark wood, that circles the room between the wood wainscot and the gold walls above. The ocher-gold color reappears beneath the table toppers for the table-cloths. Completing the picture of the old-time, old spot are the period style pendant light fixtures and the wall and column sconces that add to the ambient glow.

Sketchy artwork and simple floating shelves lined up with wine bottles and an occasional photograph break up the textured wall finish. The wine bottles become decorative accents as they are cleverly adapted to create the capital atop the column in the center of the room while other columns are converted into wine cabinets containing row after row of the available wine stock. The almost all-wood bar features another display of wine bottles as does the wall adjacent to it which is divided into cubicles in which more wines are stored. Some single patrons can opt to sit on the counter facing this wall. Sharing honors with the bar is the eye-catching pizza oven which is another focal element in the design.

Time may march on but when it comes to pizza and spaghetti—time stands still or goes backwards. At least that is the way it is at Antico Posto.

BELLA RISTORANTE

DENVER, CO

Design ▪ Semple Brown Design, Denver, CO
Photography ▪ Ron Pollard

To design the 9800 sq. ft. Bella Ristorante which is located in the Park Meadows Retail Center in Denver, CO, the firm of Semple Brown Design treated each of three elements of the restaurant as distinct entities. Though related, in the design, by "a common thread of materials and detailing," the dining area, the full wine bar and the casual neighborhood bakery can all stand alone.

A projecting steel and glass canopy serves as a visual calling card for the bakery. The bakery can be opened up to the pedestrian walk on each side since it is framed by large, custom, steel-framed, glass bi-fold doors. A focal design element in this zone is the curved entablature supported by four cherrywood columns that frame the attention-getting mural frieze which shows scenes related to baking and the bakery. The light mahogany colonnade becomes the backdrop of the bakery as well as a "detailed wood wall" in the main dining room.

Eight custom mahogany cabinets define the path that leads to the host's station. They not only show off Bella Ristorante's extensive collection of wines, they also serve as a screen between the mall and the main dining room. In contrast to the casual bakery with its black and white ceramic, checkered tile floor, the light metal chairs and tables and the cafeteria/self-serve expanse of cases and food displays, the dining room is darker and more intimate. Like the wine bar, the mahogany wood is evident everywhere: in the cabinetry, in the wait stations and the wood-backed dividers between the dubonnet vinyl upholstered

seats and backs. The richly-colored floor of wood blocks echoes the color of the trim while adding a somewhat retro ambiance to the space. Curved booths, fully upholstered in the dubonnet fabric, are backed by a grid screen of frosted white and clear panes of glass that extend up to the light ocher tinted ceiling and the mahogany crown molding around it.

"The design is one which is neither contemporary or historic in nature with a great deal of attention paid to the dark, rich mahogany millwork detailing while the plan organization is kept fairly simple providing the customer with a variety of dining options."

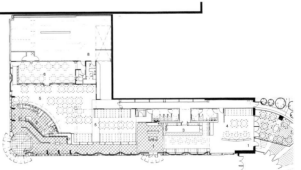

BELLA LUNA

PALO ALTO, CA

Design ▪ Total Design Group, Palo Alto, CA
Lead Designer ▪ Larry Binkley
Glass Artist ▪ Doug Brown
Special Construction ▪ Michael Trolinder
Photography ▪ John Ho

Beautiful Moon—Bella Luna—is the romantic name for the Italian ristorante that recently opened in Palo Alto—in the heart of Silicon Valley. The long and narrow floor space became the major challenge to the designers of Total Design Group, also of Palo Alto, who set out to break up the tunnellike feeling without partitions or wasting precious space.

The three-zone restaurant starts with the "common room" up front which can open onto the street and on a warm spring or summer evening becomes part of the busy street scene. The second zone—the central dining room—is framed by the columns and "flying buttresses," opposite the compact, stand-up bar, which create semi-intimate spaces by breaking up the long wall while leaving the room itself open and flexible. Away from the central zone, tucked into a rear corner, is another dining area with its own intimate atmosphere. Adding to the feeling of an Italian villa's courtyard bathed in moonlight are the faux aged, stucco walls into which are recessed green stained, hewn doors and backlit art glass "windows." Real used bricks, sawn to veneer thickness, are applied to the columns that frame the bar and stand off the opposite wall. The deep blue evening sky is painted on the ceiling and on the floor various patterns and sizes of low-fire paver tiles complete the courtyard illusion.

White opalescent glass "moons," one meter in diameter, rest on the columns and they "bathe the room in a soft moonlight glow" while the leaded art glass panels by Doug Brown "paint" a picture of a moonlit evening sky across the hewn wood back bar. A wrought iron canopy floats over the bar as well as over the interior entranceway. Hammered wrought iron is repeated throughout on door hardware, wine racks, the wall sconces and the other lighting fixtures that add to the ambient light and atmosphere of Bella Luna.

PETTERINO'S

CHICAGO, IL

Design ▪ Aria Group Architects, Oak Park, IL
Photography ▪ Mark Ballogg, Steinkamp/Ballogg, Chicago, IL

Dining and Entertainment—an unbeatable combination. Petterino's is the newest endeavor of the noted restaurateur, Rick Melman, and it is located in the heart of the growing and spreading out theatrical district of Chicago. According to the designers, Aria Group Architects, they have attempted to "evoke the feeling of a 1940's style urban men's club" that also carries a whiff of Sardi from the Broadway area of New York. The new Goodman Theater complex is only a few steps away and Petterino's was essentially designed to be the "pre-theater" hot spot early in the evening while catering to the businessmen of the area for lunch.

The corner entrance into the corner location of the restaurant is further addressed by the curved bar that

sweeps around the entry. The back bar wall is gridded and patterned with deep mahogany colored wood inset with frosted glass which is backlit to create a glowing entity. The bar itself, mahogany trimmed with red leather upholstered panels on the face, is equipped with padded bar stools finished with a red and white diamond patterned fabric. The floor here is paved with small white ceramic tiles formally dotted with maroon and black tile rosettes. The exterior bar wall is a series of double doors that open out onto a sidewalk café which makes it "the hottest (or coolest) bar in the loop after work or after theater."

The dining room setting is warm, rich and contemporary. The tile floor of the bar area gives way to wood strip flooring and the dark mahogany stained wood

appears on the wide crown molding that divides the warm, off-white walls from the same colored ceiling which is accentuated with rectangles outlined in the dark wood. Architectural piers, selected wall areas and the moldings over the red, upholstered booths continue the deep, dramatic color. The bit of wall that is visible is only a border above or below the hundreds of framed caricatures of local Chicago celebrities, musicians, and the stars who visit the windy city in their new shows.

In a smaller dining area—just off the entry and the bar—over a curved red banquette, is a mural that commemorates the neighboring Goodman Theater by MoFaux. The custom lighting fixtures that illuminate and visually enhance Petterino's were produced by The Design Development Company.

BACI

ROME, ITALY

Design ▪ Studio Ciccotti, Rome
Photography ▪ Courtesy of Studio Ciccotti

Warm, dark, colorful, intimate and so very Italian describes Baci—a truly Roman dining experience which has been designed by the noted design firm, Studio Ciccotti of Rome. Space being precious in the old Roman buildings, this small café actually resides in a pair of adjoining spaces and part of the structural, separating wall has been broken down to provide communication between the two dining areas which are served by a small stand-up bar in the rear and an enclosed kitchen behind it.

The overall palette is more than just warm and inviting; it is hot! The tired, worn, and rough textured walls of the buildings in which Baci is now located have been further aged and textured with a sponge finish in deep oranges and reds. Areas of the

old brick are allowed to show—as behind the small bar. The floor is a-swirl with a wavy pattern of yellow ocher and mustard colored vinyl that tends to break up the rigid rectangular architecture of the two dining areas. In the same design mode, Ciccotti has added an undulating cornice that extends out from the perimeter walls to become a lower and more intimate ceiling over the tables and banquettes that line the walls. The same sweeping line is repeated in a vertical plane this time as the camel back of the upholstered and tufted red booth seating. Where the separating structural wall has been removed, a diagonally-laid, dark stained wood floor is introduced to further "stretch" the architectural boundaries imposed on the architect/designer.

Dark wood timber and exposed structural steel trusses span the black painted ceiling and only the pinpoints of incandescent light—attached to the cross members—highlight the tables. The same wave motif appears as a base on the stained wood bar and it is introduced on the door that opens into Baci. According to the designer, Sr. Ciccotti, "For this project different materials were used but so adeptly put together as to create a new, stylish and trendy design that aims at interesting the widest range of clientele. Interior-wise, the place is tastefully enriched by specially researched details that add to making the ambiance pleasant and yet exciting."

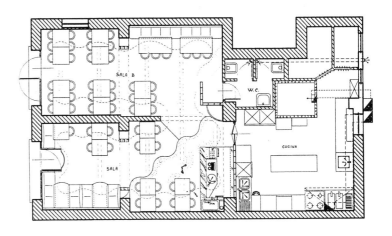

SOLE

NEW CANAAN, CT

Design ▪ Frederick Brush Design Associates,
  New Canaan, CT
Designer ▪ Frederick Brush
Project Coordinator ▪ Kevin Ligos
Photography ▪ Tim Lee Photography

In what was formerly a bank in New Canaan, CT, Sole took shape and form and emerged as a smart and sophisticated ristorante with upscale appeal— to match the smart Italian-inspired menu. As designed by Frederick Brush Design Associates, Sole combines the warmth and romance of old Italy

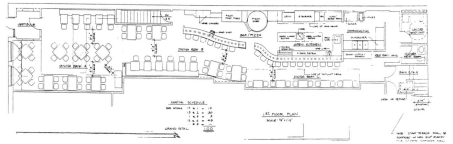

plane and cover the vertical face of the bar counter. Here the fragments of earth-colored tiles take over. Opposite the counter is a stretch of smaller booths for two with wood dividers. These tables are located under the previously mentioned "long arbor" and the skylight allows the live foliage to prosper. The show kitchen is one of the most popular spots in the restaurant and there is a wood-faced counter set in front of where patrons can sit, eat and watch the show. It is connected to the bar "which undulates with the opposing wall to break up the long length of the space."

Doric columns, faux stone work, and arched windows make up the classically inspired facade—photos of classic Italian architecture framed in recessed shadow boxes and lighting fixtures especially designed by Frederick Brush all add up to the success of the Sole design. 100 guests can be served in the 2500 sq. ft. space.

with a contemporary "now" look. To accomplish this the designer used large areas of texture and color with "no decor to interrupt the minimalist feeling of clean architectural forms."

The original space was divided into two to encompass the restaurant and a retail area. In creating the separating wall, the designer had to accommodate the existing rear skylight since it was important to the total design concept. The skylight now illuminates the "long arbor" which actually contains growing grape vines and live bougainvillea. One of the highlights of the design is the frescoed ceiling that the client requested. In previous restaurants the client always had a frescoed ceiling and he wanted the tradition to continue in Sole. According to Frederick Brush, "To carry this ceiling throughout would have thrown the balance of the contemporary and the traditional off." The solution that evolved was to have the sky, which is the background of the fresco, "shred into ribbons and seem to float away into a more contemporary space." Now the fresco seems to ripple and undulate over the gold toned space like a series of long, narrow barrel vaults that cross the length of the dining area. "What makes the space so interesting is the fact that the ceiling changes in style as it moves from front to back."

The walls are faux painted and also roughly textured with ochers, golds and salmon tones with creamy underpainting, while a rich, dark wood is used for the wainscoting. The floor is an interesting pattern of broken slabs of marble accented with tile fragments. In front of the bar, which is located up front and along one wall, the flooring materials leave the horizontal

TEATRO GOLDONI

WASHINGTON, DC

Design ▪ Adamstein & Demetriou Architects, Washington, DC
Designers and Principals in Charge ▪ Olvia Demetriou & Theodore Adamstein
Project Architect ▪ Ira Tattelman
Interior Design ▪ Michaela Robinson
Project Team ▪ Wes Blaney
Photography ▪ Theodore Adamstein

To complement the imaginative Italian cuisine, Adamstein & Demetriou, Washington, DC architects/designers, found their inspiration for the interior design of Teatro Goldoni in Venice. Using images of the theater and that magical city in Italy, the designers came up with an innovative and contemporary interpretation of what makes Venice such a romantic and magical city.

The interior design includes elegant and bold materials and added to these are "the luminous surfaces" one would expect to find as one wanders the ever surprising streets of Venice: glass, tile, stone and stucco. "The spaces are enlivened with an infusion of drama, warmth, and color complemented with Venetian glass, rich fabrics and fine furniture." The striped anchor poles that extend up out of the murky Venetian waterways and canals are given a new look in the silver and white spirally-striped columns that define the dining area along with the illuminated harlequin panels that separate one part of the restaurant from another. Over the burnt orange and mustard gold harlequin patterned upholstery of the banquettes—on the ocher colored wall—is a varied and fascinating collection of Venetian masks that also recognize the "theatrical" inspiration of the design as well as Carnivale in Venezia. The patterned floor of triangular shapes in pale apricot, beige and off-white is also suggestive of floor treatments found in the inspirational city. The loose seating, in the center of the dining room, has black lacquered chairs upholstered in apricot and burnt orange textured fabrics. A giant oval of terra cotta outlined in wood hangs down over the seating and a fanciful chandelier of turnip-shaped glass lamps is suspended off this dramatic element.

The bar stretches along one terra cotta colored wall and a giant tilted mirror panel extends across the back bar—supported by black angled rods—and in it the dining room is viewed from a different point of view. Other focal points in the design include an oversized photo mural, lit from behind, which depicts a Venetian scene as well as a display kitchen set on a stage in the center of the restaurant. Special treats are the private dining room which overlooks the cooking stage and the Chef's Table which is set in the kitchen itself and "offers an ambient and energized dining experience."

NAPLES 25

―――~~~―――

MANHASSET, NY

Design ▪ Frederick Brush Design Associates,
New Canaan, CT
Design Principal ▪ Frederick Brush
Project Coordinator ▪ Kevin Ligos
Photography ▪ Reyndell Stockman

The Americana Mall on the Miracle Mile in Manhasset, NY is an enclave of very upscale designer boutiques and top brand name shops. The affluent shoppers need a place to dine and with that target audience in mind, Frederick Brush Design Associates was invited to fashion the interiors and the furnishings for the restaurant. The result, shown here, is Naples 25—"a slick contemporary approach to an Italian concept."

To visually improve both the exterior and interior, the facade was expanded. The real attraction, however, is the wood burning oven and the show kitchen that are focal elements in the design. The kitchen is recessed beneath a series of coolly illuminated triangular-shaped ceiling forms and a frieze with a message, in Italian, from the owner: "All that you see, I owe to spaghetti." This area is clearly visible from most of the 99 seats in this 2342 sq. ft. space.

The seating options include booths for four with high backs upholstered in a blue/green/gold geometric pattern to freestanding tables and chairs out in the center of the space. The white covered chairs stand on a textured tweed carpet that subtly reunites the green/blue/gold color palette. Against a cream colored, stucco-finished wall, the high backed banquette is covered in a contemporary print with the same colors. To decorate the wall, the designer selected Italian pottery and blue glass, shadow box windows. The cool blue neon cove lighting continues around the room and eventually brings the diner's eye to the fun

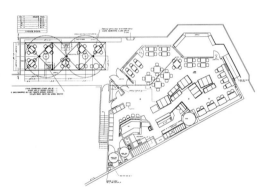

wall: a 30 ft. long plaster relief filled with Italian hand gestures executed by Nicholas Fasciano. While waiting for the classic Italian dishes to arrive the topic of conversation at the table is usually all about what those hands are "saying."

The bar is tucked into a corner of the space and small terra cotta colored alcoves create intimate dining/wining spaces for two alongside the bar. In this area the floor is tiled and the rich, warm natural wood that appears on the bar is also used on the back bar shelving. Weather permitting, there is outdoor café dining under sunny yellow umbrellas set up amid seasonal blooming plants and greenery. According to Frederick Brush, "This small location was made to look large and captivating yet kept well within the budget parameters."

IL TOSCANA

WESTON, FL

Design ▪ Echeverria Design Group, Coral Gables, FL
Photography ▪ Dan Forer

In a relatively new and developing suburb where professionals are the main residents, Il Toscana opened in the Waterways Shoppes in Weston, FL. The challenge to the Echeverria Design Group was "to create a suburban restaurant with Tuscan over-tones and ambiance incorporating a subtle Italian influenced intermixture of materials, forms, lighting and finishes."

The first requirement, however, was to make peo-ple aware of the restaurant and to do this "we used large glass windows (in the facade) so you can see into the bar and have seating up front, so it's visible when you are driving by." The problem inside came

imported Italian glass mosaics bursting with reds, oranges and yellows. The curved bar with suspended, custom-designed, green glass pendant light fixtures is centrally located in the restaurant and it is highlighted by the arrangement of the actual structural columns and the "fake" ones that were added.

According to Mario Echeverria, "Colors must be warm to whet the appetite," and there is much more to taste, savor and enjoy in Il Toscana which is rich in earth tones, deep reds, luscious golds and the accents of mahogany wood, glass and mosaics. There is much to appreciate here and it appears to satisfy the "yuppies, middle-aged patrons—well traveled and upper scale," who have discovered a bit of Tuscany in Florida.

from the asymmetrical cluster of structural columns that, in a way, determined the location and physical layout of certain areas—especially the bar." "We decided," said Mario Echeverria, principal of the design firm, "we could either work around them or make them part of the design." And they did become part of the design when faux columns were added and used to delineate the bar from the rest of the dining room.

Warm, Tuscan-inspired colors and materials take over the 5500 sq. ft. space which can seat 120 guests inside and another 70 for al fresco dining on the terrace. The space is actually divided into four zones: the entry with its semicircular walls and special seating, the main dining room, the kitchen and the bar.

The main dining room is mostly laid out with tables for two "whose settings are enhanced by the coffered and framed mahogany mirrors dramatically angled from curved, textured red walls to allow guests to gaze out throughout the dining area." The wood flooring in the reception area is accented with the same travertine marble that is used to pave the dining room floor. Paneled dividers of mahogany filled with hand colored blue, green and clear textured glass screen the waiter and pickup stations. The same strong colored glass appears on the frieze over the bar as well as over the mahogany doors and wall cabinets. The very large and very effective performance center of Il Toscana is the exhibition kitchen which actually takes up 40% of the total space. A rustic grill and a brick oven are two of the major "props" used in the "theater of cooking." Separating the kitchen from the bar is a wall featuring a flaming sun design made of

AVE. B

PHILADELPHIA, PA

Design ▪ Marguerite Rodgers Ltd., Philadelphia, PA

Ave. B, located on the "Avenue of Arts" in Philadelphia, PA, offers modern Italian cuisine with an emphasis on Tuscan flavors. To provide the timeless ambiance for this high-style ristorante, Marguerite Rodgers, a Philadelphia designer, used natural earth tones and exotic woodwork to furnish this space with its 16 ft. ceilings.

The facade has a theatrical quality in keeping with the street of entertainment venues. It features a striking glass and metal canopy topped by a marquee with a three ft. projecting "B" lit by globe lights. Inside, two antique French clocks—each seven ft. in diameter—are set against deep Chinese red finished walls and are visible throughout to remind diners of their show time. The interior has an espresso brown and black terrazzo floor, dark African wood paneling and custom, floor-to-ceiling lattice screens that separate the 88-seat casual dining area from the more luxurious main dining room which can accommodate another 82 diners. Grand columns, painted to look like parchment, are wrapped at top and bottom in rich brown leather and bound with hand forged metal straps. The main dining room is enriched by the wood framed, brown and cream upholstered banquettes, the cream leather covered, dark wood framed chairs and the gentle creamy linens. The same warm and neutral color is on the walls.

The intimate bar/lounge area features a 14-seat, dark African wood oval bar with a fluted cast concrete front and bronze lamps. The extensive selection of wines and liquors is displayed on a full height, sandblasted glass panel. The 20-seat lounge has built-in banquettes with ivory upholstery, fur covered bolsters and small hand-crafted tables. This area is defined by the wood paneling that reaches up to the herringbone patterned cork ceiling. An oval light fixture, over the bar, gently illuminates the area.

French windows framed in bronze open onto the garden café where in balmy and sunny weather 52 guests can enjoy the al fresco dining experience amid

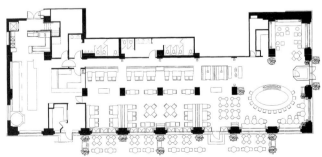

the metal trellises, climbing vines and pots of seasonal plants. Striped awnings wrap around the exterior to provide refuge from the sun. Ave. B's menu is under the stewardship of Chef Patrick Feury who traveled throughout Central Italy to taste the world famous cuisine first hand. His menu includes fresh, hand-made pastas, grilled meats, robust game and artfully created dishes using Tuscan herbs and vegetables.

BASILICO

WOODBRIDGE, ON, CANADA

Design ▪ Burdifilek, Toronto, ON
Design Director ▪ Diego Burdi
Managing Partner ▪ Paul Filek
Senior Designer ▪ Indrajit Motala
Designer ▪ Mariko Nakagawa
Technologists ▪ Tracy Morgulis /Mauro Lobo-Pires
Photography ▪ Ben Rahn, Metropoli Pictures

The cuisine of Northern Italy is prepared and served at Basilico, a 3000 sq. ft. space in Woodbridge, ON. "The concept began with the warmth of wood burning ovens, grew into a depiction of a trattoria and then a large Italian family kitchen." The challenge to Burdifilek, the Toronto design firm, was to express this inspiration in "a design language that entreats the imagination of the current age."

The contemporary trattoria is divided into four basic zones; the open kitchen where the pastas and entrees are prepared; the core dining room with a pizza kitchen; the wood ovens, and an espresso bar.

The bar and the two kitchens are stretched along one side of the space providing theater, action and entertainment. The pizza kitchen is framed in antique bronze and surrounding the ovens are rounds of actual logs—"a giddy nod to the delicious experience of wood oven baking." At the adjacent bar, diners are seated on stools and can watch the chefs working in the open pasta kitchen which has white opal glass facings and a full stainless steel backsplash. As an homage to the typical trattoria, the espresso bar is constructed of solid walnut with a natural oil finish. In addition to a marble top and bronze accents, there is a display of bottles and demitasse accoutrements.

The main dining room is filled with freestanding tables and banquettes in walnut and leather. The restaurant's cool balance of color and finish are evident here. Focal niches, carved out of the soft, neutral colored walls are used for the illuminated display of wine bottles. Overhead, the ceiling is made up of a series of "L" shaped louvers of ash planks of varying widths arranged in sequence. Sandblasted ash server stations with bianco carrera marble counter tops have the classic proportions of traditional residential kitchen work islands. Centrally placed as they are in the dining room they are subtle but colorful focal points.

Specially commissioned murals cover several of the walls with gently colored renditions of a hard wood forest, a dreamy Tuscan landscape and lemons. All these, together, "reinforce Basilico's glow of serenity and unique charm".

IL FORNAIO

NY/NY HOTEL/CASINO, LAS VEGAS, NV

Design ▪ BAR, San Francisco, CA

The up-to-date, clean and contemporary design of Il Fornaio in the NY/NY Hotel-Casino in Las Vegas certainly shows off its retro-ethnic roots. In gentle and subtle ways the designers, BAR of San Francisco, infused the feeling of warmth and homeyness into the 9760 sq. ft. refuge from the hustle and bustle of the restaurant's location in a busy casino. With a seating capacity of 370 guests, a simple plan was devised that combines an informal bar, a relaxed, neighborhood Bakery/Coffee Shop and a more formal dining room. The changes in the flooring materials lead diners from area to area.

Piazza dining on Pizza in a real, New York City style outdoor café sets the tone for Il Fornaio. The café is set out in front of the Il Fornaio facade and the tall, wood mullioned windows bring the indoor scene out to the diners on the patio. The patio is surrounded by a low brick wall accented with old-fashioned gaslight lampposts. The same casual feeling extends into the light wood millwork, wall paneling, cases and counters that make up the Bakery/Coffee Shop. Here, the floors are the old fashioned, hexagonal ceramic tiles patterned and bordered as they might have been a century ago in a local Italian ristorante, grocery store or saloon. White marble topped tables and bars and deep red vinyl upholstered seats furnish this area.

High ceilings and tall windows surround the main dining area with its sugar pine paneling and floor, the white tiled wainscoting and the partial dividers that line up the central row of booths. These are complemented by the dark red banquettes and loose seating. The relative quiet and peace of this area also contrasts with the restless activity in the casino beyond, which can be viewed through the windows. Private dining is set off from the main area in a multi-angled cove of cream colored walls decorated with numerous black framed, black and white nostalgic photographs. Overhead the ceiling is vaulted with strips of light wood and below the mini-tiled floor ties in with the Panetteria of the nearby Bakery/Coffee Shop. This area, away from the casino activity can accommodate 32 guests. The cherrywood casework is filled with the vintage wines offered at Il Fornaio.

Richness, warmth and the friendly feeling of neighborhood dining in the Il Fornaio setting makes this a top dining venue in the NY/NY Hotel complex.

RUE 57

NEW YORK, NY

Design ▪ Morris Nathanson Design, Pawtucket, RI
Design Team ▪ Morris Nathanson
Project Director ▪ Tom Limone
Project Designer ▪ Kim Nathanson D'Oliveira
Photography ▪ Warren Jagger Photography,
    Providence, RI

Rue 57 was conceived and designed by Morris Nathanson Design as a "classic French brasserie": very chic, very urban and civilized. Inspired by the all-night dining spots in Paris, this is not a reproduction as much as an adaptation to a "more uptown and tailored" type of dining experience.

The exterior provides "an extraordinary sense of theater" with the familiar Parisian storefront elements such as French doors that open onto the heavily trafficked street (weather permitting), the custom wall bracketed lights and the arresting and inviting French-style, red awnings that outline the corner location of the brasserie. The two-level interior has a large bar and a major dining room on the first level. Here there is a combination of banquettes and loose seating and to create the desired "turn-of-the-century" (19th into 20th) atmosphere the designers have used burl woods, deep burgundy colored fabrics, brass trim, areas of antiqued mirror and dozens of framed celebrity photographs. Exquisitely-detailed frosted uplights on the burl wood piers and etched crystal fluted fixtures on the ceiling were all inspired by French designs of a century ago. The ceiling is divided into dramatic rectangles by dark wood. A sushi display—in the Indo-Chine style—is set out on the first level bar which has an interior illuminated top and a back bar filled with rear lit mirrors.

The main floor has an open floor plan but smaller-

in-scale areas which are created by the careful spacing of the banquettes and furniture arrangements. Private parties are catered here and this level of Rue 57 has its own bar and "eclectic French inspired paintings provide a sense of European intimacy."

The two levels are connected by a curving stairway set off by claret red velvet drapery and the dark stained wood floors are covered with a deep burgundy carpet. One side of the staircase has a fanciful wrought iron railing while the wall is covered in small mosaic tiles in assorted wine tones. Some of the walk aisles in the restaurant are paved with miniature black and white ceramic tiles while oak floors and occasional area rugs are used in other areas of Rue 57.

RAT'S

HAMILTON, NJ

Design ▪ DAS Architects, Philadelphia, PA
Susan M. Davidson, IDC/David A. Schultz, AIA
Photography ▪ Barry Halkin

Rat's was designed to fill an elegant French country chateau that sits at one end of a sculpture park/garden in Hamilton, NJ. Designed for the noted sculptor, J. Seward Johnson, Jr., the park serves as a natural setting for Johnson's Monet-inspired, realistic sculptures which are set out amid the trees and at the artificial lakeside thus creating startlingly real tableaux. The 100-seat restaurant designed by DAS Architects of Philadelphia is divided into three intimate dining rooms, a warm, cozy and very intimate bar that can seat 12, a café/piano lounge and on the second level there is another dining area which can be used for private parties and a lounge.

A visit to Rat's is like a visit to Givergny, France but no passport is required. As designed by Susan M. Davidson and David A. Schultz, it is "an imaginative setting where people can relax and enjoy themselves" while soaking up the beauty and savoring the taste of France. The interior features solid, wood beamed ceilings and wide plank, antique cherry wood floors reclaimed from century-old barns. Connecting the two levels is a custom-made staircase with hand-milled wood railings and decorative timber brackets. Each of the three dining rooms has a wood burning fireplace that immediately suggests that warm and welcoming feeling of dining in a friend's country home. The views through the full height, multi-mullioned windows is spectacular; a Givergny-style bridge over a flower filled waterway; vast stretches of planting; trees and the beckoning sculpture garden just beyond. The rooms are decorated with distressed, custom-made round cherry tables and with wheat-backed dining chairs fashioned after those in Monet's home.

Using Monet's primary color scheme of red, yellow and blue, the upholstery of the chairs, banquettes and sofas are also ornamental accents in this

rustic/sophisticated setting. Adding to the charm and comfort are the old French limestone paved floors in the public areas, the antique Oriental area rugs that add to the color and warmth of the setting, the custom designed chandeliers and the rich, savory and gold velvet draperies with hand-fired, wrought iron rings. Each room is decorated with specially selected tapestries, paintings and sculpture—all personally-selected by J. Seward Johnson himself. The walk-in, carved limestone fireplaces were also hand-crafted at the Johnson Atelier.

Rat's was designed to be part of a "European style village." The village sits upon a circular, stone bordered driveway marked with custom-made street lamps and sculptures. The exterior of the Chateau is painted a striking shade of salmon and the deep window frames are accentuated in vibrant African blue. Also housed in the Chateau is a 25-seat wine tasting room that showcases the restaurant's 550 wine bottle selection in custom-made, temperature controlled display cases. There is also al fresco dining and drinking on the 55-seat terrace/patio which sits on the edge of the lily pond and the replica of the bridge at Givergny.

Rat's unusual name is taken from one of the characters in the children's classic "The Wind in the Willows."

LE MAS PERRIER

PHILADELPHIA, PA

Design ▪ Marguerite Rodgers Ltd., Philadelphia, PA
Photography ▪ Matt Wargo, Philadelphia, PA

Named for the traditional farm house of the Provence, "le mas", chef/restaurateur Georges Perrier calls his beautiful "country inn" located on Philadelphia's Main Line—Le Mas Perrier. To create the desired relaxed but handsome setting for his authentic and affordable Provencal menu, Georges Perrier called upon the talented Marguerite Rodgers to design his inn.

From the outside, Le Mas Perrier resembles an elegant chateau complete with slate roof tops and antique pottery urns filled with plants. The landscaping includes olive trees, hanging vines, clipped shrubbery—all "evocative of a French country garden." Inside the sprawling and spacious inn are airy dining rooms, a café/lounge, a sunlit indoor courtyard and open banquet facilities. The individual spaces are enriched with the decorative antiques and handicrafts that Marguerite Rodgers brought back after scouring through the Provence. These include 40 wooden doors, chairs, cabinets, tiered iron chandeliers and traditional pottery urns that were used to store olives and wine. Artworks, filled with the rich and vibrant colors of the Provence, also adorn some of the cream colored plaster-textured walls.

The main dining room, which can seat 60 diners, is distinguished by the 12 ft. vaulted ceilings, the large arched windows, the natural wood trim against the sunny yellow walls and the terra cotta floor tiles. The warm shades of yellow and green—associated with this sun-drenched region—are accentuated in the fabrics and the upholstery that add to the sun-filled feeling of the space. The plush banquettes, comfortable settees and chairs—copied from French originals—offer guests a variety of seating options. The yellow slip-covered chairs carry the "P" for Perrier monogram. Adding more delightful color accents are the brilliant tablecloths,

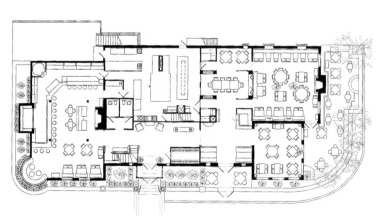

plates and the fresh floral nosegays on the tables. One of the most sought after reservations is for the Chef's Table which can accommodate 14 persons. From here guests can watch chefs orchestrate the meals through antique doors with glass windows.

In addition to this dining room there is a 30-seat indoor courtyard which features a large skylight and glass doors. This leads to a 35-seat outdoor brick patio with wrought iron furniture, a gurgling fountain and a canvas canopy over the al fresco dining area— weather permitting. A rustic café/lounge seats 40 and it offers a friendly, casual atmosphere for lighter fare, hand-crafted beers and noteworthy wines. A 16-seat, painted wood front and glazed tile bar, a stone pizza

oven and a six-seater oyster bar all contribute to the overall, relaxed social setting of the lounge area where the wooden ceiling beams and the decorative details are painted with colorful pigments that were actually imported from the south of France.

A wrought iron staircase brings guests up to the second level where the private dining and banquet hall is located. This sunny yellow, sand and terra cotta colored room can seat up to 60 guests. "Raised ceilings with exposed wood beams and striped carpeted floors give the room a Mediterranean flair." The sights and smells and the textures and colors of the Provence along with the fabulous cuisine of the area are all realized in Le Mas Perrier.

LE RELAIS

GREAT FALLS, VA

Design ▪ Core, Washington, DC

e Relais is French for "post house" or what in the American Old West was the stop where stage coaches changed horses and passenger alit to sample some of the local foods. This casual, wayside inn concept has been updated, contemporized and certainly vastly enlarged in this 4500 sq. ft. bistro/wine bar/traiteur incarnated in Great Falls, VA.

As conceived by Core, the Washington, DC design firm, it provides the "simple yet distinguished interior" requested by the client and the use of traditional, natural materials is given a new twist. Guests are invited to dine in a large, triangular-shaped room where native sandstone is used to cover many of the wall areas, the wainscoting and the mammoth fireplace that is the focal element in this part of Le Relais. The floor is laid with diagonally-aligned strips of wood highlighted with strips of a darker wood while in other areas marble tiles are used to pave the floors.

A wine rack of heroic proportions serves as a physical divider in the dining room but the open, lattice-like construction allows air and light to circulate freely. In addition to this lavish display of wines there

is also a large wine display closet-temperature controlled—and guests are invited to enter this glass, walk-in case and pick their wines from the above ground "cellar." The wine closet's construction is a geometric grid of vertical and horizontal wood strips and the same grid-like motif serves as a dropped ceiling over the wine bar located just opposite the wine cellar/closet. The bar is a combination of natural wood, sandstone paved wainscoting and pebble glass-filled dividers. Guests can be seated at the wine bar.

Framed mirrors, granite accents on bars and counters and subtly striped upholstery fabrics in muted, earthy colors on the banquettes, all contribute to the relaxed feeling of the space but it is the predominance of the textured stone surfaces and the natural wood millwork that give Le Relais its unique appearance. For those who prefer "take out," the cuisine of the restaurant is available "to go" in the traiteur located on the premises.

MIGNON

PLANO, TX

Design ▪ Knauer, Inc., Deerfield, IL
Principal ▪ Mark Knauer
Project Architect ▪ Dan Yanong
Project Director ▪ Lynn Gaede
Project Manager ▪ Amy Storm/
  Ketan Chokshi/Nadio Chen
Photography ▪ Mark Ballogg, Steinkamp/
  Ballogg, Chicago, IL

The French bistro meets the American steak house to create a unique concept: A French Steak-House. In Mignon, located in Plano, TX as designed by Knauer, Inc. "The classic steak house interior of the 1940s has been updated with a French twist to the 1960s." French sensibility is expressed in the attention to details and the use of fine materials and the graphic style of the Sixties.

Mignon is suffused in a color palette of rust, olive and gold. Dramatically upswept velvet backs on the intimate circular booths and the upholstered and tufted walls in the "cell phone" room "add continental sensuality to a contemporary look." Adding to the sensual appeal are the sweeping curved lines of the gold ceiling cornices, the sinuous line of the top of

the wood partition that divides the bistro into more intimate spaces, the round tables and the hanging cylindrical tubes of light that seem to roll over the dining area. In the bar, the cylinders hang vertically to accentuate this zone and the giant clock that fills most of the back bar is a focal element in the design.

Mondrian-style murals in textured glass of bronze, gold, persimmon, olive and amethyst and the hand painted graphics and signage "are one-of-a-kind artifacts that define the uniqueness of the concept." Portraits of icons of 1960s period in Paris such as Audrey Hepburn and Miles Davis also add to the "Left Bank" bistro ambiance.

BLEU

PHILADELPHIA, PA

Design ▪ Marguerite Rodgers Ltd., Philadelphia, PA
Photography ▪ Matt Wargo, Philadelphia, PA

Bleu, the French/American bistro and outdoor café designed by Marguerite Rodgers, adds a fresh and festive look to the Rittenhouse Square scene in Philadelphia. Distinguishing the interior of the 50-seat dining room is the whimsical mural that celebrates the City of Brotherly Love. Painted on canvas by Chris Lynn, the colorful vignettes wrap around the walls of the dining room and form a pictorial biography of the city with images of familiar places, landmarks and noted local celebrities.

The bistro is separated from the hotel lobby by a sandblasted glass partition and the walnut floors contrast with the deep navy painted wainscoting and molding trim that sets off the brilliant colors of the mural. In keeping with the bistro feeling and the indoor/outdoor concept, the furniture in the dining area consists of navy lacquered rattan chains pulled up to cherry wood and brass trimmed tables with cast iron bases. Making a strong statement, in the middle of the room, is a navy wood unit that goes from floor to ceiling and it is finished with mirror panel insets and louvered doors. Opposite this unit is the long bar

with ten stools. The black leatherette topped bar is complemented by the peacock blue upholstered seats of the stools and the back bar is almost all mirror dramatically framed with the dark blue wood—much like the three part sandblasted screen previously mentioned which stands behind the hosts station.

Weather permitting, there is a 35-seat outdoor café which is furnished with similar furniture. The large French doors are opened up and the chairs and tables face the lovely old park. Bleu features an American/French with Asian touches cuisine created and prepared by Chef Shola Olunloyo. Said the owner of Bleu, Neal Stein, "Bleu offers an exciting alternative for people to enjoy great food and drinks on Rittenhouse Square—one of the city's most beautiful parks."

PETROSSIAN

BAL HARBOUR, FL

Design ▪ Echeverria Design Group, Coral Gables, FL

It doesn't get much more French than Petrossian and that name is synonymous with gourmet delicacies, caviar, truffles and such. Now that name also shelters an upscale café/bistro in the very upscale Bal Harbour Shops in Bal Harbour, FL.

Adding all the right touches of elegance, warmth, charm and classic French chic, the Echeverria Design Group divided the 3700 sq. ft. space into four principal areas and the Art Nouveau architectural elements and original vintage artwork complete the harmonious whole. According to Mario Echeverria, "The interior decor, while certainly elegant, is intentionally restrained by the specially painted plaster walls and ceiling, mahogany wall panels, and the travertine marble flooring. The overall palette is disarmingly simple."

The main dining room area is set out beneath a domed, Gothic style ceiling and it features curved open windows. The deep, tawny gold faux painted and textured walls and ceiling affect a warm and rich glow that contrasts with the deep brown mahogany moldings and millwork and the crisp white napery. The very dark and sensuous green velvet upholstery on the banquettes and chairs is complemented by the red/violet orchids that grace each table top. This zone of the bistro can accommodate 88 guests.

Mainly a stand-up bar, adjoining the dining room, this space is dominated by the carved mahogany bar and an immense coffered mirror along with other glass details. The small lounge area in an intimate sector which is defined by brass and stainless steel curved railings and the cherry wood floor. This lovely zone provides a more private setting for entertaining, drinking, dining and is especially suited to "champagne and caviar" occasions. A specialized retail boutique, where the noted Petrossian products are available for "take home" of gift-giving, is located at the end of the dining room where the precious merchandise is exquisitely presented in cherry wood wall cabinets that are self illuminated.

Throughout, the glow of the amber glass shaded pendant lamps fill the already golden interior. Classic French posters of the 1890's, in ornate gilt frames, add to the overall Art Nouveau/ Parisienne ambiance.

CHARLO

SAO PAULO, BRAZIL

Design ▪ Arthur de Mattos Casas, Architect, Sao Paulo, Brazil in collaboration with Julia Maksoud
Photography ▪ Tuca Reines

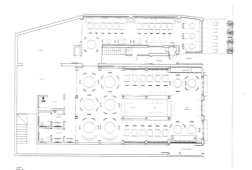

The Charlo bistro, located in Sao Paulo, as designed by Arthur de Mattos Casas and Julia Maksoud, is filled with the friendly and yet intimate feeling that Charlo Whately, the chef/owner, demanded. Charlo, the chef, is a well known and much loved character in Sao Paulo's society and this bistro that carries his name is like his home and it is always open to his friends. Who are his friends? Their pictures and caricatures line the walls of the space.

Fruity, pastel colors such as pumpkin, cantaloupe and lemon—balanced with a pale aqua and sharply accented with dramatic outlines and delineating bands of black—create the overall open and airy feeling. Windows are turned into giant black rectangles, bold black beams span across the creamy colored ceiling and vertical piers filled with panels of white calacatta marble serve to break up the long walls and create even more intimate bays for seating. Dividing the space is a large central bar and a glass partition separates the seated patrons from the kitchen which is still on view and the theater of food performance is always watchable. The floor is patterned in the gentle pastel colors of granite and all the moveable furniture is finished in black lacquer to further enhance the French bistro feeling. A pumpkin colored fabric is used to upholster the chairs.

As previously mentioned, it is the collection of "familiar faces" in large format black and white photos that really gives Charlo it's "intime" ambiance. Unposed, casual, relaxed pictures of noted residents of Sao Paulo and Brazilian "stars" fill the pale lemon tinted walls and complement the pale orange upholstered benches beneath them. These are Charlo's friends—and his guests.

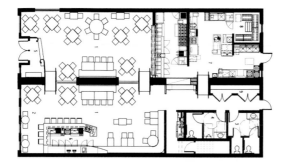

COSECHA

DECATUR, GA

Design ▪ Seiber Design, Inc., Atlanta, GA

Cosecha is the Spanish word that refers to the harvesting of the wine grapes and it is also the name of the new 3200 sq. ft. Mediterranean bistro located in Decatur, GA. As designed by Seiber Design of Atlanta, the space consists of two distinct areas—at different levels—which are connected by ramps with decorative metal railings and arched openings which allow for the flow of diners and the visual continuity between the bar and the dining room. In fulfilling the client's request for a European bistro ambiance, the designers also acquiesced and reused the old mosaic tiles that were laid in what was the former restaurant's space and also the exposed brick walls of what was the lawyer's office before the two spaces were architecturally blended into one. For ambiance, the designers incorporated colors, materials, forms and shapes associated with the Spanish, French and Italian regions on the Mediterranean.

The lower main dining room focuses on the exhibition kitchen while the raised area also has dining seating along with the bar. An "L" shaped banquette and table space for large parties is located at the rear of this zone. Existing brick and tile surfaces were uncovered, cleaned and complemented by the new terra cotta colored saltilla tiles on the floor in the bar area and the sand colored tiles with hand painted accents that are on some of the walls. The painted wall surfaces were finished in a palette that included a deep bordeaux, pale caramel and a purple-gray. The variable ceiling heights range from 8 ft. 6 in. to 11 ft. and a multi-hued, specialty paint finish was applied to the ceiling "to give the impression of an aged patina." "The unique ceiling treatment in both long, parallel rooms evokes the feel of vaulted wine cellars especially where the barrel vaulted ceiling design is articulated with mahogany beams in a raised niche at the apex." The combined dining rooms can seat 95 guests.

Nine patrons can be accommodated at the handsome, dark stained wood bar which is backed up by a framed mirror and decorative metal wine cabinets and racks. The swirling design of the wrought iron grills on either end of the bar is repeated on the railings that surround the raised dining area and suggest old Spanish balconies and their metalwork. The black covered chairs are pulled up to tables covered with a Mediterranean patterned fabric that combines the deep red color with the caramel and black.

Contemporary chandeliers and track mounted PAR 30s and 20s light up the space while pale yellow glass pendants enliven the bar surface. Warm white incandescent sconces highlight the arched openings between the rooms.

KYMA

ATLANTA, GA

Design ▪ The Johnson Studio, Atlanta, GA
Bill Johnson/Anita Summers/Karen Teske-Blue/
Sara Hawker
Photography ▪ Alan McGee, Atlanta, GA

It is hard to imagine, upon entering Kyma—a Greek taverna and ouzo bar—that is this 3400 sq. ft. space this one story building has been home to an assortment of ethic food operations and even an auto muffler shop. To set the scene for the Greek cuisine, the Johnson Studio traveled extensively and researched in Greece to find the concept which "truly authenticates the traditions of the country." The menu is prepared under the direction of Pano Karatassos, Jr. who has trained in many famous restaurants and whose father is the president of the Buckhead Life Restaurant Group-which Kyma now joins.

According to Bill Johnson, the designer, "The decor, which starts with two colossal marble columns at the entry, is an interpretation of that Greek culture aesthetic using traditional materials and imagery in a contemporary way." The space is decorated in the traditional Hellenic colors of blue and white. There is a deep blue sky painted overhead and a custom carpet in assorted tints and shades of blue—like the Mediterranean Sea—on the floor. These "rippling waves" underfoot add a subtle pattern and reinforce the name of the taverna—Kyma—which means "wave" in Greek. The white Thasos marble tiles, imported from Greece and the heroic scaled Doric columns lining the marble path are set beneath the "starlit," vaulted midnight sky which is adorned with zodiac symbols painted by Mary Frances Estock. Past the host's station is a beautifully illuminated display of fresh seafood, on ice, in a shiny white refrigerated case. Since seafood is so much a part of Greek cuisine, fresh fish is flown in daily from the Mediterranean.

The main dining room is to the left of the central aisle and net-like, semi-sheer curtains act as gentle dividers and window coverings. The white and blue checkered undercloths suggest a rural Greek taverna in this truly, sophisticated and contemporary setting. Authentic Greek "fishing lanterns" have been electrified and they provide the ambient light as well as add to the Greek atmosphere. The back-lit photographs of Greece are courtesy of Pano's cousin, Maria Karatassos, and they not only add accents of color to the white walls but they "authenticate" the dining experience. This area can seat 104 guests while on the other side of the aisle another 36 patrons can be

accommodated. The bar and lounge are on this side of the space.

The bar features small tables similar to those found in Greek kafenia or coffee houses. Wide, white grouted flagstone pavers—like those used in the Greek isles—are on the floor and a glass "curtain" behind the bar "shimmers with the many colors of the sea." Wayne and Tim Czechowski of Artwork in Architectural Glass are the artists who created this handsome panel. Also decorating the bar are the Greek "evil-eyes" which are used to ward off evil spirits. Over 60 types of Greek wines and an extensive ouzo list are available at the bar.

When weather permits, the Greek spirit moves out onto the 550 sq. ft. patio/terrace where 20 more guests can relax and enjoy their Greek Islands cruise—without packing a bag.

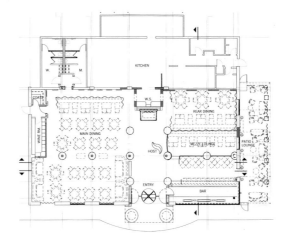

THE SHEIK

LIVONIA, MI

Design ▪ Marco Design Group, Deerfield, MI

The " flying carpet" awaits the diners—figuratively, at least—when they arrive at The Sheik where they are offered a gastronomic flight into Arabic cuisine and culture. The setting, in Livonia, MI, is a contemporary, upscale interpretation of the Islamic style of architecture. The three arches and four columns up front—clad in mahogany wood and textured stone—form the entrance way. The bronze medallions with classic eight pointed stars, symbolic of Arab culture, is introduced here and reappears throughout the rest of the café.

To capture the essence of the Arabic culture, the designers, Marco Design Group, have used materials rich in color and texture such as mahogany and stone plus old world ceramic tiles which "give texture and color to the walls and floors." Custom bronze wrought iron detailing appears all through the space and the large scale patterns of the fabrics "add a playful touch with their deep hues of Mediterranean blue, green and gold while complementing the richly textured, faux finished, gold toned walls and ceilings." To further the feeling of opulence there are custom designed tabletops with wood veneer inlays.

An authentic, mosaic encrusted, wood-burning oven serves as the heart of the restaurant. Here diners can enjoy the theater of the preparation of the freshly baked pitas. Nearby is a lavish display of fresh fruits and vegetables at the glass encased juice bar. The layout of The Sheik consists of three separate dining areas and the carpet flooring and the sheer fabrics draped over the private booths contribute to making the dining experience seem more intimate. These dining areas are clustered around the aforementioned pita oven and the centrally situated bar.

The "Arabian Nights" theme takes over the bar which is set beneath a midnight sky. Floating immediately over the bar is a "magic carpet" custom lighting fixture. Throughout the café ornamental brass light fixtures, from Syria, "reinforce the authenticity of the restaurant." Also, custom murals fill the mahogany framed walls as well as a 24 ft. long oil painting by the local artist/historian, Hashim Al-Tawil. "This blend of new materials and textures along with the collection of old world artifacts and contemporary narrative paintings of the Arabic culture bring together a warm atmosphere and setting as a complement to the total dining experience."

ALMA DE CUBA

PHILADELPHIA, PA

Design ▪ The Rockwell Group, New York, NY
Photography ▪ Paul Warchol, New York, NY

The Rockwell Group of New York City, under the direction of David Rockwell, was invited to create the look for Alma de Cuba, "a cutting edge Cuban restaurant and bar" in Philadelphia. It joins some of the other thematic restaurants owned by Stephen Starr in this area. Starr said, "The building has so many original details that remind us of the magnificent pre-Castro Cuban architecture that we knew it was the perfect location for our concept." The Nuevo-Latino menu was created by Chef Douglas Rodriguez.

The design concept was to blend the bygone spirit of Cuba with modern accents such as photographic images of present day Havana cast onto white washed walls. The facade features eight large windows with shutters typical of Caribbean housing and sheer curtains gathered by glowing light fixtures. The first view of the "action" within is through a glass partition adorned with abstract tobacco leaf imagery. Exposed brick walls, antique moldings and green mosaic tile floors are integrated into "the high energy atmosphere that pulsates with vibrant Cuban rhythms." Up front and prominent is the 58-seat first floor bar/lounge which is furnished with ultra suede covered sofas, ottomans, and dark wood cocktail tables. Red light streams through the wood slats that are suspended from the fiery red painted tin ceiling. Projected onto the walls are black and white images of Cuban people

and Havana street scenes. A colored photo is cast onto the flowing fabric that screens off the entrance to the kitchen. "The intriguing images will give the guests a feel for the much talked about country." A 16-seat bar covered with red glass mosaic tiles and Cuban style metalwork also glows with the dramatic red lighting.

The main dining room consists of custom-designed chairs and banquettes covered in off-white fabrics and chocolate brown leather. Tables of ebonized wood wrapped in artist's canvas, support flickering red oil lamps while—as a social center—there is a candle-lit, wood community table that can accommodate 12 guests. The wide wood planked floors are partially covered with area rugs that reiterate the pattern of the tile floors in other areas of Alma de Cuba. A main staircase with wrought iron railings leads up to the upper level dining room. The staircase is partitioned off by a translucent screen that features an 11 ft. projected image. "As guests enter the stair-well, bright lights cast their silhouettes onto the back of the screen." The open mezzanine dining area over-looks the busy dining room below and pyramid shaped light fixtures, inverted 3 ft. from the ceiling, add to the ambient lighting as well as the decor of the total space. The mezzanine is enriched with light boxes containing a continuous panoramic view of Cuba as well as a large skylight. Alms de Cuba means "soul of Cuba" and the "soul-food" served here is decidedly a taste of Cuba in a setting rich in Cuban-American culture.

NΛKED FISH

LYNNFIELD, MA

Design ▪ Judd Brown Designs, Inc., Warwick, RI
Director of Design ▪ Glenn M. Lepore
Project Manager ▪ Peter R. Boscio
Interior Design ▪ Rebecca Dormady
Architect ▪ Amnino Assoc., Attleboro, MA; Jefferson Group Architects, Warwick, RI
Photographer ▪ Warren Jagger Photography,

Don't be mislead by the name or the fish logo. Naked Fish is more than a seafood house: it throbs with a hot, Cuban beat all its own. As a recent winner of the *Nation's Restaurant News* "Hot Concept Award." "The Naked Fish chain embodies cultural accuracy and island whimsy in its design to provide a one-of-a-kind dining and cocktail experience."

The owners requested and the owners got the specific elements that turn this 300-seat dining operation into a bit of Latin America: the wood grill; the Latin music that envelops and lulls the diners, and the Cuban cocktails that turn the long, sleek bar into a destination. The fun feeling starts at the entrance with the dancing logo and the art deco/Miami Beach touches of color, neon and decor. Within, the space has a golden glow. Gold, yellow and ochers appear and reappear throughout: on the floor in the bar which is a decorative pattern of the assorted gold tones combined with a rich, blue-violet color, to the mustard yellow vinyl chairs that surround the bar and the simple draperies that separate the bar from the dining room. The back bar is flanked by a pair of metal sculpted frames that contain the floor-to-ceiling drapery that become the soft "columns." The internal lighting makes these two vertical elements glow. Overhead, the bar area is marked off by gold painted beams. Adding a touch-of-the-tropics are the lush plantings and trees in the large planters.

In the dining zone, the multi-gold flecked carpet on the floor and the textured gold patterned fabric

used on the high-backed banquettes are complemented by the rich, dark wood accents: the chair frames; the tables and especially the "wall" of wood louvered blinds. Simple light fixtures are suspended from the coffered ceiling and the unique "lampposts" are decorative but also add to the soft ambient light of this space.

The designers created "a space where the details exemplify the fun and energy of the food and the music" and the elements of the design are all about defining the architecture of that space.

BARCELONA

N. SCOTTSDALE, AZ

Design ▪ FoRM Design Studio, Phoenix, AZ
Principal ▪ Jose Martinez
Design Team ▪ Jay Brodala/Brent Kleinman, AIA
For Barcelona ▪ Danny Hendon, Owner
Director of Design/Construction ▪ Rick Stertz
Project Architect ▪ Nagaki Design Assoc.
Murals ▪ Artists At Large
Photographer ▪ FoRM Design team

The 15,000 sq. ft. supper club, Barcelona, opened in the rapidly developing dining/retail hub of N. Scottsdale and it has already found its niche. Seating over 400 guests, the space has been designed to host national touring entertainment. Featuring a menu of Modern American cuisine with

Spanish and Southwestern influences, the setting is also a blend of old world references with modern aesthetics "to create a dynamic environment for its upscale clientele."

The building exudes references to the Spanish Colonial architecture of the American Southwest and "historical references are captured in the symmetrical, axial layout of the grand entry." The lobby is flanked by curved wine rooms and arched passages that divide the wine rooms and lead to the private dining rooms beyond. The "crowning jewel" of this dining establishment is the centrally located, domed dining/dance rotunda. The ceiling, here, is filled

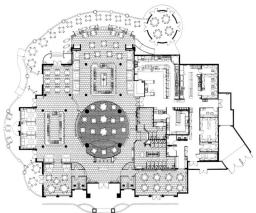

places that are not just waiting areas—but destinations in themselves. There are two bars and each features deep cherry stained millwork and warm granite counter tops. The circular bar stools, covered in amber leather, complement both the domed ceiling and the golden, faux painted walls. In addition there are the private dining rooms. The one to the west of the grand entry serves larger groups and has a private exterior patio entrance. The raised dining room is designed to be more open to the public restaurant "creating an energetic party atmosphere."

The success of this Barcelona has induced the Barcelona Restaurant Group to develop three more sites in the Greater Phoenix area tailored to the local demographics and they have begun to research the possibility of expanding nationally.

with a colorful mural of Greek gods at a bacchanal festival. There is a stage integrated at one end which is fitted with a state-of-the-art lighting system and the speakers are hidden within the draped columns. It is possible to transform the dining area into a pulsating dance floor or center of performance. Since this area is at a lower level than the entry and the East Bar—the view to the dance floor is greatly enhanced.

There is a "sense of grandeur and elegance" about Barcelona and it is captured in the high ceilings outlined with antiqued pewter crown moldings, overscaled, ornate gilded framed mirrors, and the vertical drapes that embrace the arched windows. Curvilinear upholstered sofas grouped with heavy iron and granite tables create comfortable—but lush—gathering

CINO GRILL

MARIETTA, GA

Design ▪ Seiber Design, Inc., Atlanta, GA
Principal in Charge ▪ Ed Seiber
Project Architect ▪ Mark Davis
Project Interior Designer ▪ Stacey Kirby
Design Team ▪ Lisa Sundbeck/Alicia Denton/
   Randy Miller
Photography ▪ Thomas Watkins

The client, Manana Management, requested a contemporary, energetic ambiance that complements the Southwestern influenced menu and incorporates the colors, textures and forms that suggest the Sonoran desert region. The 6500 sq. ft. space in Marietta, GA was converted into Cino Grill through the architectural and design talents of Seiber Design of Atlanta.

To simulate the architecture of the Southwest in simple, abstracted forms, the architects/designers used low curving walls, built-in planters, carved out niches and ramps and steps to affect the changes in floor levels. This also helped to create small dining clusters throughout the space. The walls are textured in sand tones and the numerous display walls, niches and surfaces are filled with artifacts and decorative objects imported from Mexico. To emulate the rippling pattern of the desert sand, the carpet in the dining area is colored purple, clay and cactus green while the upholstered booths are finished in a reptile skin pattern in cobalt and yellow-green. Two feature booths are upholstered in a copper metallic fabric accented by a deep blue suede head roll. A portion of the ceiling is open to the structure above and in the dining area a circular element, raised 8 ft. 9 in. off the floor is painted dusk red and features radiating rays that slope up from 11 to 12 ft.

The curved concrete topped bar sits on a floor of leather colored 12 in. x 12 in. porcelain tiles. A copper soffit and custom metal rack is accented by the colored lighting. The wall below the bar top is faced with sisal. The ceiling in this area is 12 ft. 6 in. and is covered with acoustical tiles for noise abatement and painted eggplant for a splash of color. The raised dining area (18 in.) behind the bar is highlighted by the backlit decorative glass around its perimeter and a framed view to the custom wine display case with the metal grid doors.

Throughout the space, colored glass and light interplay. The back lit glass artifacts and paintings are illuminated by wall mounted, low voltage picture lights on brushed metal extension arms. The bar top and back lit bar display are accentuated by recessed, adjustable low voltage luminaires and the interior sconces and pendants are blue Murano glass with incandescent lamps.

Mexican "soul food" is the menu at Taqueria Canonita in Plano, TX where the natives are close enough to the "source" so they can appreciate the real thing. The design of the taqueria by Knauer, Inc. of Oak Park. IL "reflects the contemporary interest in authentic Mexican cuisine." Here, the food is a fresh interpretation of Mexican "street food" and the interior design "mirrors the marriage of tradition with contemporary lifestyle, creating an energetic, colorful, hand-tooled yet affordable and comfortable restaurant."

To express that "authenticity," the smooth, warm pale gold walls are literally overwhelmed with dozens and dozens of assorted Mexican handicrafts: mainly authentic tin mirrors of myriad shapes, sizes and designs, custom candle sconces and Day of the Dead artifacts. In the saw-tooth wall pattern, up front, opposite the curved bar under the sweeping fascia, there are open niches filled with more decorative Mexican handicrafts and ceramics along with inscribed snatches of Mexican poetry. The sleek wall finish contrasts with the strongly grained, native mequite wood that is used for the tables and the bar.

TAQUERIA CANONITA

PLANO, TX

Design ▪ Knauer, Inc., Oak Park, IL
Principal ▪ Mark Knauer
Project Architect ▪ Dan Yanong
Project Manager ▪ Lynn Gaede
Project Specialist ▪ Amy Storm
Photography ▪ Mark Ballogg, Steinkamp/
  Ballogg, Chicago, IL

The V-shaped benches set into the zigzag wall are covered with deep brown leather-like fabric and trimmed with nail heads—as are the booths further back in the main dining room. The rectangular mirrored panels, grouped and mullioned like "windows" reflect the myriad decorative elements on the opposing wall. Hanging down from the blacked-out ceiling are inverted, truncated, cone-shaped rawhide covered lamps that add more to the golden glow that washes over the tables and the stained concrete floor.

Weather permitting—and usually it is most agreeable—the casual, outdoor patio offers another seating option. Partially covered overhead and illuminated by dozens of strung lights, this area is filled with verde gris finished metal chairs and tables with stone inlaid table tops, and plants in planters, on pedestals and suspended from overhead.

LEFT AT ALBUQUERQUE

SANTA BARBARA &
SAN FRANCISCO, CA

Design ▪ BAR, San Francisco, CA

The special attraction in Left at Albuquerque's traditional Southwestern fare—in addition to the "healthy and natural" ingredients—is the fun feeling that fills these spaces designed by BAR of San Francisco. Each restaurant is uniquely tailored to fit into an existing building (preferably old) and the bar is always the focal element in the design. It is faced with corrugated metal panels and there is the signature tequila rack over the bar. Wood is used for the wainscoting and other warm and earth friendly wood finishes are incorporated along with the wrought iron railings, lighting fixtures and accents.

The designers go "hog-wild" when it comes to punctuating and pulsating the space with color. Strong bright primary colors appear on the patterned and solid seat coverings used on the banquettes and chairs while a refreshing lettuce green shares the wall surfaces with a happy cream color. The wood floors are planked with timber and hanging from the "vintage" pressed metal ceiling are unusual pendant light fixtures. Between the wood beams that crisscross the silvery ceiling are the equally shiny HVAC ducts and pipes that are far from hidden. The structural columns are enhanced and given prominence as they sprout natural timber limbs that reach up to support the ceiling beams.

The Santa Barbara 3775 sq. ft. facility is located in an historical building on State Street. 73 guests can be seated in the main dining area with 25 more in the cocktail/dining area off the bar. The bar itself can accommodate 12 guests and for al fresco dining 20 persons can be served on the out-of-doors patio. In contrast, the San Francisco Left at Albuquerque is

located in an upscale neighborhood off Union Square and can accommodate 100 guests. A skylight, in addition to the large windows that face out towards the street, adds daylight to the café's lighting plan. As in Santa Barbara, the walls are loaded down with assorted artifacts and accessories such as vintage posters for Old Westerns, period advertisements, gasoline and antifreeze cans, neon outlined clocks, metal signs that originally graced old country stores and highways and other "road kill" such as hub caps, headlights, and hood ornaments. Anything and everything goes to create a festive and fun dining experience and enhance the Rte. 66 flavor of Southwestern cuisine.

Targeted at the middle to upper income suburban families and couples, the 7000 sq. ft. freestanding Firebird's Rocky Mountain Grill brings "the hearty tastes and warm rustic lodge appeal of the Colorado Rockies" into an Old English village-themed suburban shopping center in Charlotte, NC. The architect/designers, Little & Associates were truly challenged to merge the two different feelings into something compatible with both.

The building's ashlar stone veneer and synthetic stucco was used in traditional details to convey the quaint exterior village feeling while the white washed wall trellises and sloped roof design elements were used "to create a more rustic form language without diverging from the shopping center's Old English style." To add a feeling of warmth and welcome, gas lamps appear at the entry and in the bar. To draw guests into this "Aspen lodge," the clerestory windows of the entry tower "glow in a lantern-like manner."

FIREBIRD'S ROCKY MOUNTAIN GRILL

CHARLOTTE, NC

Design ▪ Little & Associates, Architects, Atlanta, GA
Photography ▪ Prakash Patel Photography

The central focus of the three dining areas, which form a sort of amphitheater, is the "stage" which is the expo kitchen. This focal area is highlighted with ovens, rotisseries and wood burning grills which provide assorted sensory stimuli of smells, sights and sounds. The open, soaring and spacious dining room features heavy timber cross beams and trusses that sweep over the area and under the wood planked ceiling. The beams and trusses are supported by mighty, barkless tree trunks that, combined with the stone and steel "create the rustic, comfortable dining atmosphere." These heavy timbers supported by the aspen logs and exposed rusted steel columns "emphasize the craftsmanship of the material connections."

Dry stacked and rock-faced synthetic stone plus rough sawn, rift-cut wood paneling also add to the "rustic" look.

The lounge/bar area features a wood burning, stone fireplace and a rusted steel-faced bar. A hanging stained glass and wood light fixture hangs over this area with its lower and more intimate ceiling which is finished with wood planked floors and furnished with natural wood tables and chairs. The back bar is gently illuminated from a light cove above which accentuates the stony textures of the walls. Gas light lanterns on the field stone piers and columns add to the lovely, low level of illumination in this area.

PINTXOS

SAN FRANCISCO, CA

Design ▪ Allied Architecture & Design,
San Francisco, CA
Roddy Creedon/Martin Austria, Jr./Michael Chen/
Erin Lilly/John B. Lin/Lih-Chuin Loh/Jeshua Paone
Photography ▪ Allied Architecture & Design

A former retail appliance store was transformed into the new tapas bar/café, Pintxos, in San Francisco. The designers/architects, Allied Architecture & Design, retained the century-old texture of the existing floors and the wood structure since they provided a quality that would accentuate the newly introduced surfaces of steel, resin and glass tiles. As designed, there is now "an interplay of a highly eclectic existing structural system with a set of new, more ordered counterpoints and framing devices." Steel moment frames in a cross direction and layers built up from the long sides of the space "act to figure a set off overlapping rooms that weave together old and new, street and alley, steel and wood."

A pair of colonnades made up of simple rusty metal columns topped with timber separate the drink and tapas bar from the casual floor seating and these constructions create a strong axis down the length of Pintxos. The bars are faced with glass mosaic tiles in yellows, greens and blues while frosted glass lighting fixtures in yellow and blue are suspended over the bar. The same cool, fresh palette of refreshing greens appears on the walls and ceiling and the upholstered, high backed banquettes set into niches formed by architectural piers. Light, natural rattan seats and

backs are used on the chairs while molded plastic chairs (yellow in color) are pulled up to the tables with tops made of material salvaged during the demolition stage of Pintxos. Some of the furniture has also been reconstituted from this salvaged material.

Halogen MR16 lamps are recessed in the green tinted ceiling, attached to the wood timber colonnades and hung down, as necessary, to light up the artwork on the walls. They add bright accents of light but also create the soft overall level of illumination in the café.

EMERIL'S

ORLANDO, FL

Design ▪ Morris Architects, Orlando, FL
Managing Principal ▪ Gerald Koi
Design Principal ▪ Walt Geiger
Designers ▪ Jim Pope/Gary Altergott/Scott Martin
For Emeril's ▪ Emeril Lagasse/Tari Lagasse/
　Eric Linquest/Martin Dalton
Architect ▪ HOK Studio E, Orlando, FL
Photography ▪ Raymond Martinot

meril Lagasse—but more frequently recognized as just "Emeril"— is a household name to anybody who loves food and is addicted to watching him perform his culinary magic on The Food Channel. This 11,700 sq. ft., two-story restaurant in Orlando, FL is the fourth such venture for the food star.

"As in Emeril's preparation of food, the sequence of arrival, host greeting, procession to the bar, rooms, tables and seats is carefully controlled to heighten the experience of the meal as well as the experience of the dining place." A warehouse structure is the basis of the design and the two levels are organized on a straight line cutting diagonally across the trapezoidal building plan and ending by the bars. A 2 1/2 story high open dining area and the porches are set on one side while the two VIP dining rooms, cigar room and wine rooms are on the upper level. The restaurant boasts a 10,000 wine bottle collection which is contained in glass enclosed wine racks that are located throughout the space: hung

from the walls, freestanding, framing the corridors and positioned under the stairway.

A special feature element in the design is the exhibition kitchen and food bar which serves as an "on location" venue for network telecasts of Emeril at work. Also on the main level are the main dining gallery, a wine bar and a main kitchen which has a VIP table within it. The lower level wine bar and the upper level wine catwalk, placed in glass forms, serve as a bridge element between the main dining gallery and the street. The porch dining "serves as an extension of the dining gallery onto a large urban piazza."

To enhance the warehouse feel of the setting, Morris Architects relied on natural materials such as wood, brick, stone, glass and steel. Maintaining and promoting the "natural" quality of Emeril's art are the exposed tongue-and-groove pine ceiling beams, the patterned oak and maple wood flooring and the raw, black iron railings of the connecting staircase and railings around the balcony. As Walt Geiger, principal at Morris Architects, said, "The goal was to create a background to showcase the food so that the food is the star." Thus, using materials, colors and textures inspired by the seasonings, spices and herbs featured in Emeril's rustic style of cooking, the colors range from the oyster white shells in the entry to the gold and paprika spiked millwork.

Because of the high ceilings, the custom two-way light "ceiling" was lowered on industrial conduit to create a light plane for the table tops. Intimate spots highlight each table and uplights illuminate the clerestory "to create a beacon which radiates through the clerestory and on to the piazza."

FRANGIPANI

MUMBAI, INDIA

Design ▪ *Virgile & Stone, London, UK*
Photography ▪ *Courtesy of the Designers*

The design concept for the Frangipani café in the Oberoi Towers in Mumbai, India is a fusion of Indian culture and contemporary details: Indian crafts and imagery encased in a modern, simple architectural shell which not only appeals to international guests but to the local clientele as well.

The designers, Virgile & Stone of London, based the layout of Frangipani on the principals of the theater where "food is the main device to create an active and exciting, all embracing environment." Action stations replace the "traditional counter barriers of the open kitchen" and now the preparation and the presentation of food becomes the central attraction point. A highlight of the area is the platinum finished state-of-the-art pizza oven. Two long banquette seats form the central spine of this room which can seat 120 guests. These lead the diner's view towards the end wall which carries an eclectic collection of contemporary objects and Indian artifacts. This focal wall is another major decorative statement in the design and a deep blue light washes the background of the artifact display "to create a more intimate and softer ambiance." A 20-meter long etched glass—behind the

three action stations—is patterned with the names of native herbs and spices engraved in English and Sanskrit. The Frangipani logo, in a combination of vibrant colors, reappears throughout the café's design.

The white Calacatta marble on the floor of this 450 sq. meter space is combined with Indian sandstone around the action stations, dark oak chairs and paneling, etched glass and accent colors of deep purple and burnt orange on the drapes to "create a welcoming, light, airy and tranquil place to relax away from the heat of the day." The long and narrow exterior terrace alongside the café creates interesting vistas for the diners and tends to extend the interior space beyond its real boundaries. Out on the deck of Indian sandstone and timber, the actual Frangipani trees grow in giant pots and add their color to the café's design concept.

DASAPRAKASH

SANTA CLARA, CA

Design ▪ *Akar Studio, Santa Monica, CA*

The diners know that a new epicurean treat awaits them as soon as they arrive at the 1970's style strip mall. The unique storefront, designed by Akar Studio, breaks from the neighboring shopfronts with the promise of something exotic and different. The entire restaurant is revealed through the tall rectangular windows that are divided by a composition of ribbed glass and copper panels framed by dark bronze mullions.

The vegetarian cuisine of Southern India is presented in an ambiance of natural colors, rustic textures and modern forms. The feeling is evident in the entrance atrium which features a rectangular copper clad element filled with floating flowers and candles. The sculptural metal partition above this trough "abstractly depicts the design theme of handmade artisan craft work" that appears again and again within the restaurant. The divider consists of rough surfaced metal squares mounted on steel tubes arranged horizontally in color from copper to verde gris.

Throughout the space there is the distinct contrast between the colors that make up the palette such as muted greens, earthy yellows and bright reds and shocking pinks. These colors are "evocative of both the colorful melange of spices used in the Southern Indian cuisine as well as the bright, festive fabrics of traditional dress from this region." Some of these embroidered silks are used decoratively: draped over wall mounted hooks on soft yellow tinted walls.

The dining area is distinguished from the entry/foyer by the maple wood flooring that replaces the mottled tile. Booths are set along one wall and

they are replayed in the recessed rectangular mirrors set in the opposite wall. Soft, unobtrusive downlighting brightens the mahogany-surfaced tabletops that are scattered throughout the space and the lighting also highlights the artisan craft elements and "draws out the warm, sunset colors of this design." One of the focal elements in the design is the window recess with four boldly-lit masks which are traditionally used in the dances of the region.

In addition to the design of this dining room Akar Studio created the colorful menus, business cards and stationery "ensuring a unified vision behind all the restaurant's design elements."

TOMMY TSUNAMI

DENVER, CO

Design ▪ Semple Brown Design, PC, Denver, CO
Photography ▪ Ron Pollard

Located on the street level of the Larimer Sq. Parking Garage in Denver's historic lower downtown district —now an entertainment center—is the 6600 sq. ft. Tommy Tsunami. An intricately detailed but very eclectic Asian theme has been veneered over the exposed concrete structure to create an exciting and energetic gathering and eating place. According to the designers, Semple Brown Design, the space is organic in plan and "organized around a series of events."

One of these "events" is the Sushi bar which is centrally situated and accentuated by a skeletal canopy of fir wood blades. Pendant lights hang over the polished concrete bar top to provide a warm and enhancing glow. A curved, cast-in-place low divider topped with cylinders of light serves to divide the sushi bar from the drink bar area which is another "event." Beyond the bar are a series of private dining rooms separated by shoji screens. They feature on-the-floor seating atop tatami mats. The central "events"—in the main dining room-are the teppan grills and the open kitchen—"these events integrate the showmanship of Asian cooking."

Contrasting throughout with the cast-in-place concrete and steel are the vertical grain, fir wood elements which "soften and unify" while adding a feeling of warmth to the space. Also integrated are a variety of lighting techniques and thematic elements such as

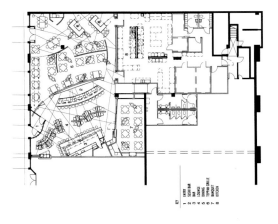

KEY
1 ENTRY
2 SUSHI BAR
3 BAR
4 LOUNGE
5 DINING
6 TEPPAN GRILLE
7 BANQUET
8 KITCHEN

the Ninja motorcycle which is now part of the back bar, the custom paper lanterns, stylized shoji screens, elongated Japanese stock market displays and a video wall. According to the designers, "The design of the individual elements within the space make subtle references to classic oriental textures, patterns and compositions, as the steel and wood divider walls are reminiscent of lattice screens and wood fences."

All in all, a fun, action-filled space with an eclectic Asian/Pacific Rim theme-with a menu to match.

MORIMOTO

PHILADELPHIA, PA

Design ▪ Karim Rashid
Photography ▪ David Josepha

As a setting for Chef Masaharu Morimoto—the Iron Chef of TV fame—Stephen Starr, the noted restaurateur, commissioned Karim Rashid to create a space that would blend traditional Japanese design with organic and sensual elements. The result, shown here, is a design to awaken and stimulate all the senses.

The symmetrical design features geometric booths with glass dividers extending down the length of the space while smaller versions, for two, create a border along either wall. Large amorphous shapes and soft egg-shaped sculptures emerge from the smooth, white plastered walls above these more intimate booths. The glass partitions, that create a pattern between the staggered booths for two to four diners that form the spine of the main dining room, are electronically controlled and they change color so at one time the space will be flooded with an emerald green glow and then switch to a fiery red. The colored glass tables with white leather benches/booths can accommodate 125 diners. The yellow glass, box shaped sushi bar can seat another 15 but the guests seated throughout the room can also appreciate the artistry and theatrics of Chef Morimoto and his staff.

Twenty-two feet overhead is an undulating ceiling and the floor below is laid with dark brown bamboo strips. Nestled between the waves of the ceiling is a mezzanine level and an intimate VIP room which can seat 30. White leather banquettes border the perimeter of the room and the bar is a glass unit glowing with an amber light. In addition there is another private room which can accommodate up to 16 guests and here the communal table is recessed into the floor recalling traditional Japanese dining. "Magically lit, the enclosed space glows in soft light," and that can be said of all of Morimoto.

POD

PHILADELPHIA, PA

Design ▪ The Rockwell Group, New York, NY
Photography ▪ Paul Warchol

This "futuristic" Asian restaurant on Sansom St. in the U. of Pennsylvania campus in Philadelphia was designed by David Rockwell and the Rockwell Group of New York City. It was fashioned to set the stage for the extraordinary Asian/Fusion cuisine. Into this all-white setting, the designers have added lots of theatrical devices including lighting effects, a conveyor belt sushi bar and unique dining "pods."

The ultra modern, space age design has been executed with unexpected materials such as molded rubber, sculpted plastic and smooth resin and foam sculpture for lounge seating—not the usual materials one finds in traditional dining rooms. Adding to the unconventional seating for 90, in the main dining area, are the high gloss white epoxy walls, the creamy white concrete floor and the acoustical foam ceiling. It is the bold, bright and colorful lighting that really takes over. "The whole space is white—like a canvas—and all the color comes from the lighting," said Kimberly Silvia Hall, senior designer at the Rockwell Group. In keeping with restaurateur Stephen Starr's passion for the 1960's fun culture, the ambiance is retro-futuristic.

Pink light washes over the white acrylic tables decorated with brilliant bursts of color and the communal table with white foam chairs for 16 guests. For "more intimate" dining there are seven "pods" that

seat two. Three private dining "pods" are set on one side of the space flanked by the sushi bar and the bar/ lounge. These are available for larger parties and feature white upholstered banquettes and walls with a wraparound, clear glass window. Once inside the "pod" the guests may choose from nine switches as to which colored light to illuminate the area. "The interactive, glowing 'pods' create a visual delight for guests throughout the restaurant." A 44 seat "pod" shaped dining room is used for private parties and it is enclosed by a sliding glass door. This area is set at the rear of the main dining room and is separated from it by a "curtain" of silicone tubing with pink and white acrylic rods.

Burnt orange light glows hot and steamy behind the oval sushi bar which can seat 34. A conveyor belt, along the top of the white bar, delivers fresh sushi directly from the kitchen. A 60 in. video screen, above the sushi bar, shows nonstop animated Japanese cartoons. Pale blue light cools off the bar/ lounge where up to 50 guests can indulge themselves seated upon Martian red foam sculptured seats. The 14-seat bar has a translucent amber resin bar top lit from beneath with white neon.

Stephen Starr said that Pod is like something "you've never seen before, yet there is familiarity. It is very groovy, like a cocktail party at the Jetsons."

THE PEARL

NANTUCKET ISLAND, MA

Design ▪ CMS Architecture & Design, New York, NY
Principal in Charge of Design ▪ Chris Smith
Project Designer ▪ Julia Roth
Project Architect ▪ Claire Moore
Photography ▪ Scott Jones

It is hardly what you would expect it to look like! An early 1880's Federal-style, three story building on Nantucket Island is home to The Pearl—a restaurant that features Asian/ Fusion cuisine. The restaurant is located on the second and third levels and take up a total of 4000 sq. ft. A centrally-located staircase links the levels and the salt water fish tanks, enclosed between the pale blue cabinetry above and below, serve as unique focal elements in the design and also refer to the source of the cuisine.

"The space was designed around the motion of water," said Chris Smith, principal in charge at CMS. "The space reflects the calming and illusive qualities of 'light and water.'" Tints of blue are painted on the walls and millwork while natural pine flooring adds to the clean, contemporary Nantucket look. The ceilings are painted a soft pink and some areas are covered with a pearlescent fabric. The banquettes that stretch along the soft, sheer draped wall are upholstered in a cream colored, pearlized leather which adds yet another gentle shimmer to the overall ambiance of The Pearl. A fireplace wall, roughly textured with used bricks, makes a dramatic contrast to the rest of the space.

Throughout, the lighting is soft and subtle. The illuminated salt water fish tanks provide the ambient light with halogen MR16 lamps used as accents. Blue gels are used over the "hidden" fluorescent lamps that back light the sheer draperies and the onyx bar top is also back lit. Said Chris Smith, "The client wanted an updated fresh approach to the Nantucket traditional dining experience"—and that is what they got! The two private dining rooms, on the top level, offer "a personal service and look." One is the "warm" vintage wine room and the other is the "cool" springtime pink room. The Chef's Table, just off the kitchen, is a fun location while for "intimacy and romance" there is the deck overlooking the side garden.

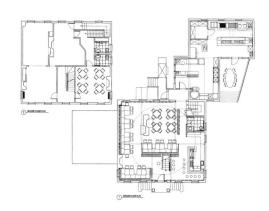

YANYU

WASHINGTON, DC

Design ▪ Adamstein & Demetriou Architects,
Washington, DC
Principals in Charge ▪ Olvia Demetriou/
Theodore Adamstein
Project Architect ▪ Frank Beltran
Interior Designer ▪ Michaela Robinson
Project Team ▪ Wes Blaney
Photography ▪ Theo Adamstein

Adamstein & Demetriou, Washington, DC based architects, were invited by Jessie Yan, Vanessa Lim and William Tu—the owners of Yanyu—to "create a restaurant that captures the serene elegance of high Asian culture through inspired cuisine and bold inventive design." According to Theo Adamstein, "We were asked to draw on the richness of traditional Chinese architecture and design, interpreted in a reduced contemporary language."

The existing two level space on Connecticut Ave. NW, in Washington, DC had an unusual and irregular footprint. A new fire-rated stairwell had to be inserted along with an opening in the floor "to help connect the two levels both physically and visually." Using stone, dark wood and stucco each dining area was designed to have a distinct and unique character— "from dining along a busy urban street window to the intimacy of the booths on the upper level to the bustling Chef's Table located near the kitchen." A back lit panel of three layers of silk covers a large part of the fire stair and it "echoes images of Chinese sailing ships." To create a clear, cultural reference and also add some color and detail there are two large murals: one of the emperor and another of the empress. Throughout the space, a simply patterned grill of wood slats is used to unify the spaces. The grid serves to partially obstruct the view from the street through the large glass windows that surround two sides of the space and as vertical dividers between the booths on the upper level.

Glowing lanterns, sculptural lights carved into the mural walls, wall-washed surfaces and backlit silk panels all add to the warm and sensual glow that creates the desired atmosphere of Yanyu. "The ambient lighting is flattering, soft and complements the architecture and the diners." Dining at Yanyu is a "sensual and atmospheric dining experience."

KOSUSHI CAFÉ & BAR

SAO PAULO, BRAZIL

Design ▪ Arthur de Mattos Casas, Architect, Sao Paulo
Collaborator ▪ Silvia Carmesini
Consultant ▪ Gilberto Elkis
Photography ▪ Tuca Reines

A Japanese café/bar in Sao Paulo, Brazil? Why not! It appears that there is a large Japanese community living and thriving in Sao Paulo but it has only been during the past two decades that the Japanese cuisine has caught on and become a cuisine of choice among the natives and visitors to Sao Paulo.

Located in a simple, three story concrete construction, the architect/designer, Arthur de Mattos Casas, decided to use that "concrete box" and fill it with " a few but strong interior design elements." The 6400 sq. ft. space is neither Japanese or Brazilian in theme but a subtle blending of the two rendered in clean, contemporary lines. The designer's concept was to create a warm and cozy atmosphere by using basically Brazilian furniture of the 1950s and 60s. Native Brazilian wood is used on the floor and bamboo and tatami matting—in recognition of the Japanese cuisine and ownership—is used on the ceilings. Natural, native fabrics upholster the seating.

One of the visual highlights of the design is the use of the picture panels of the original passports of the sushi chef's grandparents. They reside in places of honor in the sake bar area. The photo enlargements have been gently restored and tinted a soft sepia by Tuca Reines who also photographed this project. In this area of Kosushi the black lacquered chairs are imported from the US but covered in local fabrics of pale melon, apricot and gold. The sushi bar is separated from the sake bar and it adjoins the kitchen.

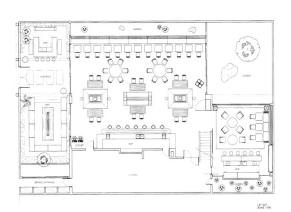

The black base and stainless steel top of the sushi bar are complemented by the gently-illuminated panel of Japanese characters set out above the bar.

The many windows are covered with bamboo shades and tatamis that also recall the Japanese heritage and tradition. Skylights, set into the wood grid that frames the tatami matted ceiling, add daylight to the interior. A garden, just outside the long wall of banquette seating, is another delight. It is filled with Bonzai plants and stone sculptures. A modern touch is the four sided, metal tubing etagere which holds the 16 TV monitors. Japanese cartoons from the 1950s, '60s and '70s play on the screens while in an adjoining cabinet there is a collection of Japanese toy

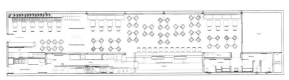

BENIHANA

LIMA, PERU

Design ▪ Metropolis, Lima
Architect/Designer ▪ Jose Orrego
Photography ▪ Jose Orrego

enihana of Tokyo is an American franchise operation with locations around the world. One of the most recent incarnations has been in the Jockey Club Shopping Center in Lima, Peru. The design by Jose Orrego of Metropolis, in Lima, makes effective use of the 600 sq. meters of space which is actually two dining rooms in one: a sushi bar and a teppanyaki.

The dining experience starts at the entrance where diners are invited to go through a rock garden and over a little lagoon with a Japanese water clock. Once inside, the corridor has a wood ceiling that is inspired by those found in Shinto temples. The traditional style sushi bar has a chef behind it and stools with red leather-like seats lined up in front of it. The same red material covers the base of the bar and it is distinguished by a frieze of wood fretwork backed by with rice paper illuminated from behind. Mirrored panels and wood shelves appear on the back bar and decorative paper lanterns hang down over the bar and light up the area as well as bring attention to the corner location.

In the teppanyaki or grill area—there are 12 tables that each seat eight guests who have come to be entertained—and fed. These tables feature grills set into the table top and black hoods hang down over the grills to vent the smoke and some of the

aroma. Here the chefs stand at each table and make a "show" of the slicing, dicing, chopping, seasoning and stirring of the foods on the work surface and the grill. The black granite topped tables are framed in the same reddish brown wood that is used throughout the restaurant. The red Benihana logo appears on all sides of the black venting hoods.

There is also a U-shaped bar for drinks with a highly polished and varnished wood top. A dropped ceiling, over the bar, combines panels of red set into a wood grid with wood slats to hold the glasses above. Surrounding the dining room are exhibit cases filled with kimonos and decorative ceramics and sculptures. All the lights in the space are controlled by an electronic dimmer system.

HARU

W. 43RD ST. & BROADWAY
NEW YORK, NY

Design ▪ Tony Chi & Associates, New York, NY
Principal in Charge ▪ Tony Chi
In Charge of Lighting ▪ David Singer
FFE/Purchasing ▪ Tammy Chou
Project Director ▪ William Paley
Architect ▪ Tobin & Parnes, New York, NY
Photography ▪ Kelly Bugden

The combination Japanese restaurant/sushi bar and bar that opened just off Broadway in the heart of New York City's theater district was designed by Tony Chi & Associates to "serve as an intimate 'neighborhood' destination." 110 guests can comfortably be accommodated in the 3100 sq. ft. space which offers "tranquility, psychologically distant from the noise and hustle of New York's most busy commercial district."

A wall of silver leaf sets the look for Haru right at the entrance. The multilevel design scheme is soon apparent when guests have a choice of sitting out in the open on maple chairs pulled up to cherrywood topped tables or opt for more secluded seating in booths crafted of solid walnut. Antique bamboo mat partitions (5 ft. x 5 ft.) are used to organize the arrangement of the booths each of which has its own pendant lighting fixture. The main dining room is "an inviting and cozy sunken space" with concrete flooring. This space is delineated by the birch tree trunks that fence in the area on four sides.

Alternating light and dark ceramic tile flooring surrounds the sunken area with birch tree "fencing" on three sides. The poured concrete "coffered" ceiling "accentuates the well-ordered, modernist character of the restaurant." To the left of the dining room is a western style cocktail bar with stainless steel and solid rose-

wood furnishings. The bar itself is distinguished by an overscaled collage of antique bamboo matting, black river stones, mirror and large format, black and white photographic images of Tokyo in the 1950s.

The sushi bar "is a vital focal point providing a bit of visual theater." The back wall of this bar is surrounded by a silver leafed arch and the wall is covered with hand made, green glazed ceramic tiles. The textural appearance is due to the tiles being rectangular in shape but triangular in section. The ceiling, overhead, is covered with black and white newspaper print that complements the black and white tile flooring and the distinctive oriental style furniture.

"Haru is about warm, generous hospitality. It is about intimacy. And it is about ultimate comfort and relaxation."

HARU

~~~~~~~~~~~~~~~~

PARK AVE.

NEW YORK, NY

Design ▪ CMS Architecture & Design , New York, NY
Principal in Charge of Design ▪ Chris Smith
Project Designer ▪ Julia Roth
Project Architect ▪ Claire Moore
Photography ▪ Scott Jones

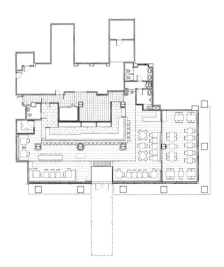

Haru is a chain of Japanese restaurants/bars and shown here is another branch of the chain also in New York City, but visualized by a different architect/design firm. Chris Smith, principal at CMS Architecture & Design said, "The space was designed around the notion of Springtime since that is what 'haru' means. Springtime was the departure point for the design concept: dappled light, greens of every shade, lightness, water and air."

The concept and layout was in response to the client's request for "an updated fresh approach to lunchtime dining as well as flexible space for evening diners." The sliding wood screen in the layout provides privacy for private parties as well as flexibility in seating arrangements. To create the desired ambiance, the designers used a palette of yellows and greens that were painted on the walls and ceilings. The surprising floor treatment is a larger-than-life photographic mural of fresh blades of grass protected by layers of polyurethane. Recycled plastic and paper is used on the windows "to filter the daylight and illuminate the windows at night." The wooden benches that serve as banquettes are "softened" with cream colored leather seat pads and the same recycled paper/plastic fabric used on the windows is air filled and used for the back rests. Spring green vinyl upholstery is used on the loose seating. The focal fish tanks are illuminated and that soft light is combined with halogen MR16 lamps. A custom glass chandelier hangs over the communal dining table in the center of the space.

The over 60 ft. long bar/sushi bar is covered with a continuous bas relief of Corian material which was first used on this project. A supersized original calligraphy painting by Tsuru is on the back bar while fish tanks with "robotic fish" serve as playful eye distractions for the diners.

P.F. CHANG'S CHINA BISTRO

LAS VEGAS, NV

Architecture & Design ▪ MBH Architects,
Alameda, CA
Photography ▪ Andrea Brizzi

P.F. Chang is a familiar name to people who enjoy good Chinese cuisine and the Chang China Bistros appear in many cities across the USA. This award-winning design (*Chain Store Age* competition) is located in the very new and very exciting Aladdin Hotel/Casino in Las Vegas.

Since the long and narrow space of P.F. Chang is located between the casino and the "heavily themed facade" of the hotel, the client along with MBH Architects of Alameda, "modified the interior and exterior elevations to create a thematic bridge between the contemporary Chinese influenced restaurant design and the strong Arabic character of the resort." What was originally conceived as a single level unit developed into a four level design. In addition to the structural problems inherent in that change it also meant that the increased dining capacity would require the restaurant to expand downward into the two levels of the sub-grade parking garage.

Skilled millwork and metal craftspeople worked in close conjunction with the architect and the client to design, detail and fabricate the exquisite cherrywood booth enclosures, the hanging panels and the wood wall paneling and the dramatic winding wood, brass and glass staircase that links the two dining levels. The wall stone tiles are in variegated golds and blues-"deep and saturated exemplifying the sumptuous nature of the restaurant." The heroic scaled molded plywood and acrylic pendant lights add not only light but add focal interest to the overall look of the design. They hang down from the vaulted ocher colored ceiling and illuminate the black lacquer topped tables set out on the rich, russet floor. The booths are lined up under the mezzanine dining level and they are upholstered in a handsome, jewel-toned fabric while a red curtain blocks off the dining areas above.

The aforementioned grand staircase is located at one end of the large dining room and set against the multicolored stone wall. The second level not only contains a large, central dining room filled with cherrywood panels and a fretwork ceiling of wood but there are private dining rooms as well. Rich red walls and red patterned upholstery plus lovely Chinese ceramics displayed in wall niches set the scene for lavish private Chinese-style banquets. Fabric drapes, along one whole side, offer the desired privacy.

Another focal feature in P.F. Chang is the small curved bar recessed under the mezzanine. It is highlighted by the cutout and illuminated ceiling and the back lit wall which has been geometrically divided—a la an Asian Mondrian—into areas for bottle storage and the display of Chinese artifacts and arts. This P.F. Chang takes up 14,000 sq. ft. and is part of the 62 restaurant chain.

NOODLES

LAS VEGAS, NV

Design ▪ Tony Chi & Associates, New York, NY
Principal in charge of Design ▪ Tony Chi
Photography ▪ Paul Warchol

In describing this project which can seat 75, the design firm said, "Located along the path leading to the mythic high stakes gaming room, a modest Asian café winks at you with a bold expression: the ancient Zen tradition always defining and celebrating form of entry with plank. This gesture stages the experience to be unveiled."

It really does start out front with a minimalist facade dominated by a giant bundle of noodles hang-

ing over the entry way. The noodles-like signage—
dominates the doorway while a video monitor to one
side—in the dark wood paneling-illustrates the menu
and the kinds of noodles available. Once inside, the
patron is gently assaulted with noodles of every shape,
size, and color presented in glass containers artfully
arranged on glass shelves framed with the dark wood
which are cantilevered off a backlit, white frosted wall.
The "noodle in a jar" motif is repeated throughout the
warm, glowing interior. The designers selected noodles from around the world and " celebrated (them) in
their respective glass containers in a trophy fashion."
On the opposite wall, where the diners sit, are hand-
made artworks generated from the "elements" of noodles in their raw form. The diners sit at long, natural
wood, communal-style tables such as those that are
typically found in noodle houses in Asian countries.

The "operatically staged" display kitchen is at the
far end of the room and directing the guest back there
is the white floor patterned with "dancing Chinese calligraphy" spelling out noodle recipes. "At the dining
counter one can see sumptuous noodle dishes cooked,
garnished and finished at this cooking theater and
then making their way to the audience seated in various groups through the restaurant".

As envisioned by Tony Chi and his team this
"comfort food café" is casual and contemporary but
"the Bellagio has a very unique setting—unlike a lot of
other casino floors—it has a very elegant design. We
didn't want this to feel like just any coffee shop." And
it isn't just another coffee shop. This award winning
design was called "a masterful design" by the judges
who also praised the use of accent and display lighting
which not only enhances the overall ambiance but
shows off the art and artifacts that give texture and
meaning to the total design.

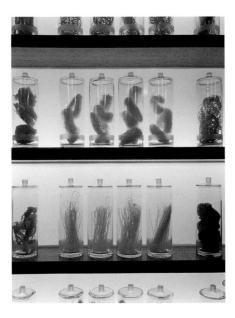

ast met West and the meeting took place in Schaumburg, IL where Mark Knauer of Knauer, Inc. came up with a new/old concept: an Asian diner. It is noodle shop meets fifties diner and the result is a true winner.

The exterior of this Asian Diner is sharp and contemporary in styling with gridded elements that recall shoji screens and the crisp geometry can be anything-even an updated diner. Black fish-eye windows pierce the stone textured side walls but the "giveaway" is the vibrant red, overscaled, big rice bowl with giant chop sticks that becomes the logo and the signage for the diner.

Inside, a palette of red, amber and black appears throughout: in the fabrics used as drapery to separate dining areas; on the vinyl upholstery for the wood encased booths; and on the chairs that pull up to the freestanding tables. The same palette appears on the highly lacquered red shutters over the open kitchen, the millwork walls and partitions and the stained concrete floors. The exposed ceiling is painted black and highlighted with wooden beams patterned with

BIG BOWL

SCHAUMBURG, IL

Design ▪ Knauer, Inc., Oak Park, IL
Principal ▪ Mark Knauer
Project Architect ▪ Dan Yanong
Project Manager ▪ Ted Flis
Project Specialist ▪ Mayur Modi
Photography ▪ Mark Ballogg: Steinkamp/Ballogg

Chinese fretwork designs. Large "streamer" fixtures—like three glowing amber "pancakes" of light—hang over the seating area and in front of the open kitchen. Similar light fixtures, used vertically, appear atop the wood dividers between the booths. Another fun Asian touch is the wall papered with oversized Chinese and Asian currencies which have been greatly enlarged and cleverly collaged to become part of the red, amber and black color scheme. The rich orange toned wood is used throughout the design to tie the elements and areas of the design together while adding its part in turning an American Diner into a Chinese styled bistro.

According to Mark Knauer "These dramatic elements are carefully arranged to provide a visually exciting yet flowing environment in which to enjoy the equally exciting and alluring cuisine."

DEL FRISCO'S
STEAK HOUSE

NEW YORK, NY

Design ▪ Aumiller-Youngquist, Chicago, IL

el Frisco's Double Eagle Steak House, in Dallas, ranks with the very best in steak houses across the country. When a spacious, two story space became available in midtown Manhattan Del Frisco's felt it was the time and place to join the other great steak houses thriving in New York City.

Aumiller Youngquist, the noted Chicago design firm, was entrusted to redefine the steak house concept for today and create a design that was not only suited to the client but to this city as well. The 16,000 sq. ft. space is located in the McGraw Hill building, just opposite Rockefeller Center and the Radio City Music Hall and only steps away from Broadway and the theater district. According to Bill Aumiller, a principal in the design firm, "The restaurant is situated on what is quite possibly the best restaurant location in the country." The 30 ft. ceilings and fabulous full height windows not only add to the spacious feeling but light strains in during the daylight hours and at night the pedestrians on the street are treated to the sights within Del Frisco's. "We've created a space that is truly unique to its location and guests can relish the hustle and bustle of one of the world's greatest cities while relaxing in a tranquil setting".

That setting is filled with rich, dark wood paneling on the walls and projecting piers that contribute strong vertical accents to the already stately space and play up the heavy timber beams that angle out from the central row of columns and contrast with the light ceiling. These "beams," which create a series of "V" shapes, actually carry the uplights that illuminate the ceiling and the light that is reflected down is the ambient lighting for the restaurant. One of the major focal elements in the design is the truly "grand" staircase that angles and sweeps guests up to the mezzanine seating. The wonderful wrought metal railings also become the balustrade around the upper level dining area. Tucked under the angled turn of the stairway and the mezzanine is the dramatic "old fashioned" mahogany bar which is enriched with standing lamps on the bar top. Gray slate is laid on the floor around the bar and black leather bar stools are pulled up to the black marble topped bar.

The upper dining area is more intimate but just as warm and rich. The mahogany wall paneling continues around the curved wall which is partially covered with an heroic-sized mural. Amber tinted glass lamps top tall black metal bases to become contemporary torcheres that complement the myriad recessed spots in the ceiling. Black leather upholstery is used on the banquettes along the wall and on the loose seating as well. Here,

the floor is covered with a gold and taupe patterned carpet. Also on the mezzanine appears to be what seems to be a "must" in the steak house setting"—the cigar room. In Del Frisco's "cigar room" glass covered and individual wood cabinet humidors line one wall and the big, poufy "masculine" easy chairs are covered in dark green leather. Small mahogany side tables and reproductions of "fleshy female" paintings add to the clubby, "old boy's club" feeling of the room. There is also another, smaller and more intimate bar on this level set under a ceiling with beams radiating out from over the bar. An elevator brings guests down to the wine cellar and here, under a recessed vaulted ceiling a smaller dining room is filled with hundreds of wine bottles nestled in the cubicles and arched wall cabinets that line two walls of the room.

According to the designers, "The result is a design which is completely extroverted to fit the spirit of the city rather than introverted as in the original Del Frisco's, celebrating as much the city of New York as it does the dining experience."

GREENWICH
STEAK HOUSE

GREENWICH, CT

Design ▪ Haverson Architecture & Design,
Greenwich, CT
Jay Haverson/Carolyn Haverson
Photography ▪ Paul Warchol

When one speaks of Classic American cuisine—
something a bit more upscale than diners and
"comfort foods"—it is "steaks and chops." To
recreate that wholesome, hearty and "traditional" look for the Greenwich Steak House,
Haverson Architecture and Design's team of designers
under Jay Haverson, designed "a classic steak house
with a past." Extensive renovations were needed to
transform a former dining operation into what is now
not just another steak house.

The concept was to "tell the story of the town of
Greenwich by surrounding diners with Greenwich as
it was in a bygone era." This was accomplished
through the use of beautifully framed, sepia tinted
historical photographs on rich, mustard colored walls
with an antique white trim. "Greenwich's colorful history provided the perfect way to connect the restaurant to the heritage of the people who lived in the
town." The over 50 photographs, culled from archival
files of the town's Historical Society, include war
heroes, athletes, authors, and artists as well as estates
and street scenes that no longer exist.

The diner enters into an "historical" setting: a vintage butcher/retail meat counter and a grand bar that

says "look back diner." The bar is antique in look: all dark wood enriched with moldings and cornices especially on the woodwork on the back bar. Viridian upholstered bar stools are set out on the stained, "worn" wood planked floor in the bar area. The dining options include several rooms or areas that lead from one into the next. "The colors were reworked to have a more authentic and substantial look" and black and oxblood are the major furnishing/accent colors. According to the Haversons, "The look is masculine in feel, with classic architectural touches to tie together elements of the bar, the wainscoting, freestanding columns, an open sweeping stair and wide plank wooden floor finishes." Vintage style chairs and tables and banquettes—upholstered in oxblood—and the opulence of the padded and tufted wall formed by the sweep of the stairway all contribute to the overall ambiance.

The Harvest Room is reserved for private parties and/or guests seeking a quieter and more intimate setting. The low vaulted ceiling, fireplace and lamp shaded chandelier are enhanced by the display of the steak house's wine collection. In addition, there is a café/lounge on the second level which, on weekends, turns into a nightclub featuring live music.

SMITH & WOLLENSKY & WOLLENSKY GRILL

CHICAGO, IL

Design: Haverson Architecture & Design,
  Greenwich, CT
Principal in Charge of Design: Jay Haverson
Principal in Charge of Administration: Carolyn
Photography: Paul Warchol

Situated overlooking the Chicago River and nestled between two 60-story circular towers that are so much a part of Chicago's skyline is Smith & Wollensky Restaurant & Grill. The challenge for the designers, Haverson Architecture & Design, was to incorporate the same stylistic vocabulary, color palette, lighting details and signage from the New York Smith & Wollensky steak house operation and still make it personal and unique to Chicago—and make it fit in with the organic modernism of its location.

The restaurant is an elongated, octagonal shaped structure with a slightly canted roof with a central skylight. The roof is lead coated copper and it echoes

the neighboring building behind it. Inside, guests have a choice of two dining options: Smith and Wollensky for a hearty meal and libations or Wollensky Grill for lighter fare. Smith & Wollensky, on the lower level, has its own bar and a series of seating areas that are private and distinctive within the overall space. Seating options include banquette areas, a series of booths, open seating dispersed throughout and a platform for special "dignitaries." The upper level dining has the feeling of an open bistro. The interior design of all the dining options includes remembrances of things past and decor "that recalls the social atmosphere and warmth of an Irish pub "with dark stained maple wainscoting, green marble banded chair rails, and buttery yellow painted walls. There is even an antique, brick-faced fireplace to complete the illusion. The ceilings are flush acoustical tiles but the sprinklers and some of the plumbing pipes and electrical conduits are left exposed "as if to say this is an establishment that might have been here before modern architecture prevailed." Personally selected by the client is a collec-

tion of antique bulls, bears and eagles along with beautifully framed paintings of the same bygone era. There are even prints of Chicago's famous World's Fair of the 1930s. On the stair landing between the two levels is a cleverly arranged "family" of carved bears bearing plaques honoring such Football Hall of Fame Chicago Bear greats as Mike Ditka, Dick Butler, George Hallas, etc. "The artifacts are elements that help to define the space as a distinct Chicago establishment."

According to Haverson, "As intended, we captured the old world charm and character of the New York eatery, but to our satisfaction recreated it in such a way as to make it more personal and unique to Chicago."

TELLERS RESTAURANT

ISLIP, NY

Design ▪ Soffes Wood, New York, NY
Photography ▪ Peter Paige Photography, NJ

Imagine a wine cellar in a steel barred vault. Imagine dining in a space where tellers and depositors exchanged friendly greetings and money matters under a soaring coffered ceiling. Imagine a time before the ATM machines and impersonal banking services. Visualize these tall

windows set in the classic architecture of a 1920s bank building, allowing light to stream in over happy, prosperous suburbanites in the pre-Depression days. Not only can you experience it but savor it as well while dining on the American cuisine now being offered at Tellers in Islip, NY.

Tellers is a 7000 sq. ft. bank building of that long gone time that has been rehabbed into an upscale dining establishment. The classical style exterior facade, with unusually tall proportions, large Ionic columns on the side and a hip roof with acanthus leaf details, is still a proud landmark in this town. The idea of the owners was " to create a relaxed atmosphere—not formal or traditional—as a special destination for dining and family events." Under the creative stewardship of Soffes Wood, the

architects/designers, the dropped ceiling that was added in the 1950s was removed and the height of the main dining room is "absolutely the most dramatic element of the design." The 35' windows , spaced between the exterior columns, the long draperies and the wall sconces "define the main dining room and fill the shell with warmth and sound absorbing quality." Though the space is open and airy, the designers have filled it with luxurious touches such as an aubergine carpet and soft brown banquettes that "ground" the space. These colors contrast with and balance the warm eggshell color on the walls and the linen draperies. Dark wood chairs tie in with the "warm" ambiance.

A unique feature of Tellers is the Cigar Bar which has richly stained anigre wood walls and a hand-

some bar constructed and finished in walnut with patinaed copper trim. Providing the "clubby," intimate and human scale to this room are the upholstered seating, the traditional light sconces and the wood slatted Venetian blinds. Framed black and white photographs are used to decorate and personalize the room. Small private parties can be accommodated in smaller enclosed rooms under lowered ceilings. Some are furnished with wood burning fireplaces, deep salmon velvet covered chairs and mahogany tables. These deeper toned rooms with their wood strip floors turn family gatherings into special events. In another area, away from the soaring, coffered ceiling, flexible freestanding tables can be reconfigured for private parties as well. Here the deep toast colored walls are covered with dozens of framed pictures, photographs and artwork.

A new reception area added and the entrance to Tellers is at the end of a landscaped path through a terraced garden. The garden is furnished with benches, garden ornaments and beds of seasonal flowering plants. As previously mentioned, not to be missed, is a look into the original vault of the bank that now serves as a temperature controlled room for Tellers wines and a humidor for cigars.

GREENWOOD

WASHINGTON, DC

Design ▪ Core, Washington, DC
Principal ▪ Peter Hapstack, lll AIA/IIDA/ISP
Principal ▪ Dale A. Stewart, AIA
Team: Dave Conrath/Kathleen Clare Ngiam/
  John Musolino
Photography ▪ Michael Moran Photography,
  New York, NY

In a rich, dark, romantic and earthy setting filled with natural materials and textures, a new/old kind of dining experience awaits. Set down in the heart of sophisticated Washington, DC is Greenwood, a restaurant designed by Core for Carole Wagner Greenwood. This is her third restaurant and as Peter Hapstack, of Core, explained, "Carole was looking to move her cooking closer to where her clientele lived and in coming to this residential area, the decision to emphasize community dining is a natural one."

Prominently located in the center of the "barn like" setting is a long, community table that seats 22. The table is framed by a natural wood sculpture suspended by cables. "The design focuses on creating a community dining experience nurtured by a home made, organic and artistic atmosphere." Guests are seated next to other diners they may or may not know and on this long, natural wood table share in the American cuisine prepared by Ms. Greenwood. Custom made, blown glass lamps hang throughout the space and over the table creating a glowing ambient light while also highlighting the artwork by local artists.

The millwork throughout is crafted from recycled wood: rough cut and left unfinished "to bring out the texture of the material." The ceiling has been left open in the center of the dining room to reveal the original stamped tin ceiling of the 1930s vintage building that now houses Greenwood. Many layers of red paint coat the walls to give it the warm, worn and weathered look that so enhances the space and the dining experience. According to Hapstack, "There's a little bit of found architecture, a little bit

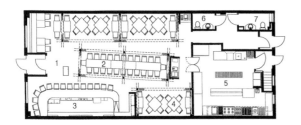

of creative architecture, a little bit of reused architecture and a little bit of new architecture. It is all part of the hand crafted atmosphere we wanted to achieve".

The Hostess' stand and the architectural arbor it stands in are constructed of 100-year-old wood reclaimed from a dock in Chesapeake Bay. The translucent draperies that hang from the arbor can be drawn around a seating area to create "a defined space without walls." To one side of the entrance is a 15-seat bar with a pine front and limestone tile top. Hand finished photographs by Colby Caldwell adorn the back bar wall. Another special touch is the menus which are inserted into old cookbooks from the Chef's personal collection. They make nice browsing material for those who don't want to get into the community feeling.

"The materials, textures and colors engage diners during their visit. They are comfortable in their familiarity but are treated in a modern, sophisticated way."

ANIMATION CAFÉ

ATLANTIC CITY, NJ

Design ▪ Daroff Design, Philadelphia, PA
Architect of Record ▪ DDI Architecture
Photography ▪ Elliot Kaufman, New York, NY

Within the bold swirl of sharp, clear colors, metallic finishes, and sweeping, turning shapes and forms is the newly redesigned, 24 hour café in Bally's Park Place Hotel/Casino in Atlantic City, NJ. This undulating and convoluted plan not only can seat 380 guests, it also contains Mr. Ching's Chinese Restaurant. By the combined efforts of Daroff Designs, Inc. working with DDI Architecture, "The contemporary environment is enhanced by the angular dining counter and wall openings, modern light fixtures and undulating wall surfaces."

Within the space, diverse seating options are available and the choices include areas of intimacy or those more open to the spectacle of the surroundings. According to the designers, the space is "animated" with exciting colors and forms. The strong, multicolored carpet and the splashy contemporary fabric used to upholster some of the booths are balanced by the large, solid areas of vibrant red, teal, violet and peach. The banquette backs are defined by sweeping curves and the wood chairs have violet fabric covered seats with oval backs of natural wood or stained burgundy and terra cotta. Atop the table bases that were there from before, are solid surface table tops with spots and specks of red, violet and gold within a white matrix. "A whimsical feeling is created in the seating areas which features booth and chair arrangements set below "floating" soffits and that feeling carries through to the supporting columns that run the length of the corridor. The columns look like silver wrapped cones being unwrapped-or being stretched to reach the ceiling height. Sliding doors and walls were added to Mr. Ching's so that part of the space can be used during the daylight hours as part of the café/coffee shop service. At night, there is a separate entrance that leads to Mr. Ching's where the Chinese-style menu is served.

To differentiate the spaces and yet keep the unified feeling there are openings "cut" into the curving partitions that provide both privacy and still a feeling of community. Playfully designed glass chandeliers in bold red, green and blue are used to delineate spaces while in the main, loose seating, area the lighting fixtures create starburst patterns on the ceiling.

FIRE & ICE

PROVIDENCE, RI

Design ▪ Prellwitz/Chilinsky Assoc., Cambridge, MA
Principal in Charge ▪ David Chilinsky, AIA
Project Architect ▪ Mark Connor, AIA
Interior Designer ▪ Susan Greco, IIDA
Designers ▪ Derek Rubinoff/Christopher Brown
Photography ▪ Anton Grassel

It's all in the grill, and grilling is the thing! Prellwitz/Chilinsky Associates followed up on their first successful Fire & Ice restaurant with this sensational 10,000 sq. ft. project in Providence, RI. The challenge, as before, was to design the space so as to allow for an interesting but directed circulation flow so "diners can understand how the interactive dining system works without confusion." Diners are invited to go through the various stations where they pick up and pile up the fresh ingredients that they then bring to the focal grid where the food is prepared.

According to the designers, "The free-wheeling, as-you-like-it dining approach to this innovative restaurant is boldly expressed in every aspect of the restaurant's design. A kaleidoscopic scattering of light, color and errant geometrics visually integrate the spirit of spontaneity and creativity that is central to the interactive dining concept." The 10 ft. circular grill is central to the physical layout and the interactive concept of Fire &

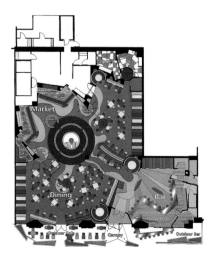

Ice. It radiates beams of silver, copper and gold up to the ceiling 24 ft. over it. The satellites around the grill include the salad bar, the sauce bar, and the ingredient markets. Imagine the visual cacophony of 24 bright and scintillating colors all colliding in a kaleidoscopic collage: blues, reds, violets, oranges and chartreuse. Each wall reaches out in a different color and texture and the textures vary from wood strips, corrugated galvanized sheet metal, to plastics and plaster finishes while carved-out niches in the walls add "to the richness of surface." Contributing to the overall sense of excitement and theater are the metal laminates, metallic paints, floor tiles and rubber floors, vases, tomato vine cages used in unusual ways as lighting fixtures and the numerous other design details.

According to the designers, "The restaurant is a sculpture in itself. Huge, open-ended, cone shaped volumes create private dining nooks. Changes in scale, texture, color and light boldly collide every few feet." This definitely is "the fresh, visual environmental experience" the client asked for.

MOVENPICK PLAZA

ZURICH, SWITZERLAND

Design ▪ Tony Chi & Associates, New York, NY
Principal in Charge ▪ Tony Chi
Project Manager ▪ Jefferson Lam
Project Designer ▪ Stewart Robinson
FFE ▪ Tammy Chou
Lighting ▪ David Singer
Photography ▪ Morley von Sternberg

Movenpick Plaza, in Zurich, is a new café designed by Tony Chi & Associates of New York City to serve as a prototype for Movenpick Untemehmungen as an extension to their hotels and resorts. According to Tony Chi, "The restaurant is to be viewed by its patrons as the place to choose when seeking the casual and comfortable. It is for the fun part of the Swiss society." In addition, the 147-seat operation is distinguished by a high level of quality and there is variety in its services.

There are basically two dining options: the café or the full service dining room. To establish the Movenpick patron-friendly and service-oriented qualities, leather wall panels, at the entrance and into the café are decorated with images of the parent company's products and the people who produce them. They immediately establish the desired "friendly

atmosphere in a relaxed setting." The rich, tawny leather covered walls are complemented by the warm toned, highly patterned wood floors, marble and figured wood table tops and the off-white upholstered chairs with natural woven leather backs. A refreshing touch in the café is the line up of countless olive oil bottles on the open back shelves which forms a dividing screen. Yellow plastic panels, decorated with words in assorted graphic type faces, are used to shield the fluorescent lamps that illuminate this area.

Zebrawood veneer appears on the chairs and is used to highlight the service stations in the main dining room though the woven leather backs and light covered seats remain consistent for the chairs. A white marble counter separates the kitchen from the restaurant but the copper canopy over the counter and the visible areas of mosaic tiles on the back wall of the kitchen and the colorful spices piled up in the

tall glass containers on the counter top all help to bring the kitchen area into focus for the diner. Complementing this counter is the long drink bar—covered in the same white marble—and here the back bar is filled with shelving of the same richly patterned zebrawood. Panels of multi-green glass mosaic tiles line the niches in one wall of the dining room and these are fitted with tall glass containers filled with fresh fruits.

A long mirror with a beveled frame fills most of another pale yellow wall and it echoes views of the loose seating, the low marble partitions. The lighting plan, created in-house, creates the desired ambiance. "It is subtle enough that it creates a relaxed tone, yet lively enough that all are not put to sleep." Movenpick Plaza is "simple, natural and welcoming" and the flexible design created by Tony Chi & Associates keeps things vital, fresh and vibrant.

CAFÉ BISTRO

**NORDSTROM
DEPARTMENT STORES**

Design: Engstrom Design Group, San Rafael, CA
Photography: Courtesy of Engstrom Design Group

nvisioned as a casual café—a family-oriented dining experience that would appeal to the sophisticated Nordstrom's shoppers—Café Bistro is the newest dining concept being introduced into some of the Nordstrom stores. The 3500 sq. ft. restaurant includes an active display kitchen and seating for 120 guests.

The concept of an open kitchen in a department store setting is new and the Engstrom Design Group of San Rafael has managed "to provide a dramatic visual connection to the food" while reducing the square footage required for in-store restaurants. The working counter, adjacent to the entry, is the patron's first point of interaction. The counter in front of the cookline serves as a pivotal, multifunctional area where customers can order (or dine), waiters pick up entrees and desserts are prepared and showcased. Bold colors, organic shapes and natural materials "reinforce the idea of fresh, high-quality food that is available fast." The angular checkerboard design of green, pale rust and white fills the back wall of the display kitchen and the muted green ceramic tiles that surround the oven also face the front of the serve-line/counter. Pull-up high stools are provided for persons who prefer dining at the counter and watching the action up front. The venting hoods, over the cookline, keep the aromas inside the restaurant and out of the retail sales areas of the store.

Most of the café has been rendered in a warm, neutral palette of natural colors and textures. Color accents have been introduced in areas where they can be "updated" without a major remodeling such as on the painted soffit and the graphic window treatments. The distinctive, sofa-like curved upholstered booths, backed up by swirls of walnut, are covered in a soft green fabric—the same color that is used in the kitchen area. A contemporary geometric pattern in rust, beige and brown is used to cover other banquettes and the booths lined up along the perimeter wall. Dark brown wood appears on the chair backs and seats of the pull up chairs. A swirling, tendril-like pattern in the green marble tiled entry and the cookline area sinuously complements the other gentle curves in the total design and also leads the diner to the basket weave carpet in the seating area.

Custom lighting contributes to a sense of energy and drama that is well differentiated from the retail area" and the hanging, leaflike dropped elements in speckled gold tones combined with the vibrant earth colors on the curved soffits make this a most pleasant place to stop, to sit, to sip, to eat, and prepare for the rest of the shopping experience.

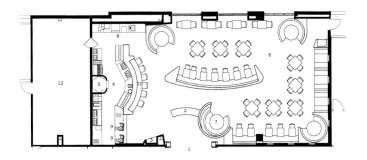

DE KAS

AMSTERDAM,
THE NETHERLANDS

Design ▪ Piet Boon
Concept/Owner ▪ Gert van Hageman
Photography ▪ Kees Stuip

In 1926 the city of Amsterdam constructed a giant glass structure in which exotic plants were grown and the area surrounding the greenhouse served as a nursery for trees to replenish the city's parks. Years went by, the greenhouse fell into disuse and eventually disrepair and finally was scheduled to be demolished in 1997. That is when Gert van Hageman stepped in to save the structure and with the idea of turning it into a café. It took a few more years until the EAT Construction company started to rebuild the building with basic elements using jack plugs and rivets. With reverence and respect for the original design and construction, the interior designer, Piet Boon, had prefab elements made that matched the original designs and details. With a perfect eye for just those details, Boon carefully selected the materials, finishes and furniture, the decorations and the exotic plants that once again are blooming in the greenhouse.

The restaurant is about 1000 sq. meters in size and can accommodate 50 persons inside and another 60 for light dining and aperitifs on the terrace. White concrete floors and off-white upholstery on the banquettes and pillows for the black mesh chairs combined with the crisp white painted woodwork contrast with the black wall that sets off the kitchen/service area from the dining space. Natural wood tables are lined up under the fabulous peaked ceiling of glass and steel. All the metal framework in the soaring space is painted black as are the long horizontal tubes that run the length of the structure carrying the HVAC systems.

In two smaller greenhouses, attached to the main structure, the chef's have access to home grown fresh vegetables, herbs, spices and such. Fruit is grown in an orchard, also on the grounds, and "everything is bred with respect to the environment" and in keeping with the changing seasons.

The author/editor would especially like to thank the photographer of this project, Kees Stuip, for bringing de Kas to our attention.

LEGAL SEA FOODS

WEST PALM BEACH, FL

Design ▪ Elkus Manfredi, Boston, MA
Principal in Charge ▪ Howard K. Elkus, FAIA, RIBA
Project Manager ▪ Joseph M. Carroll
Project Architect ▪ Brent Zeigler
Team ▪ Lou Bancesco/Aliza Shapiro/
Chris Walters/Justine Wobbe

The client, Legal Sea Foods, Inc. of Allston, MA selected Elkus Manfredi of Boston to establish their look in West Palm Beach, FL. The architects/designers found their inspiration "under the sea," a likely space for great fresh fish food.

The space is divided into several distinct areas. The focal point in the central dining room is the gleaming, stainless steel abstract sculpture of seaweed and fish by David Tomlinson. The area itself is defined by curved mahogany walls, and "ribs"—suspended from the ceiling—suggesting boat structures. Adjoining the central seating is the gallery. Another boat form is suggested here in the mahogany vaulted ceiling. One side of the gallery consists of multi-paned windows and on the opposite wall a bold, Adam Cjanovic painted mural of lighter blue-green images suggests a broad, breaking wave. This leads the eye to the gallery's dramatic water wall of backlit, stainless steel, sinuous wave sculptures also by Tomlinson. The sculpture is set off by translucent glazed, wood framed panels which also define the gallery end as a more private dining area.

A third dining option is the al fresco terrace—under a large, yacht-like awning. The bougainvillea bordered area overlooks the steps that connect the adjacent cinema court with the main plaza of City Place below. The bar is dominated by another large scale Cjanovic mural executed in deep blues and greens "evoking underwater turbulence." The liquor display is surrounded by the blue and white tiles that are a Legal Sea Foods design signature.

Stone and carpeted floors, plantation shutters and mahogany furniture upholstered to complement the overall blue and green palette along with the bubble glass lighting fixtures are all used to enhance the marine theme.

UNDER THE VOLCANO

〜〜〜〜〜〜〜〜〜〜〜〜〜〜

NEW YORK, NY

Design: Tree House Design, Ltd., New York, NY
Jack Baum/John Van Der Linden
Photography: Peter Paige

The intimate, 1400 sq. ft. bistro/lounge in the Murray Hill section of Manhattan takes its name from a book written by Malcolm Lowry. Within the context of a rather unhappy story, "The small space was designed to convey the importance of drink at that time and place in history." Since the story is set in Mexico in the period between the two World Wars on the Day of the Dead—a religious celebration— "without extolling drink as a religious experience, the space had to convey that sense of reverence to alcohol portrayed by the main character and the story's underlying theme: control of one's self versus destiny."

The storefront has randomly placed panes of amber stained and textured glass set in a steel framework which becomes a visual barrier between the sidewalk and the bar. Dominating the exterior is the oak bar and the enormous, oak framed, beveled mirror over the back bar. Pilasters, edged in hand made, glazed ceramic tiles, surround the mirror. Rare and premium tequilas—a specialty at Under the Volcano—are displayed in the internally-illuminated, hand-painted wood vitrines on the face of the pilasters. The surrounding tiles are Mayan-styled with a bas relief design executed in a chocolate brown.

The floor is covered with recycled, salvaged oak planks with a natural finish. Jack Tree, of Tree House

Design, selected a wood wainscot to surround the perimeter and it has been faux painted to affect an aged and distressed look. Three self-lit, wood display cases are built into this wainscoting and they are used to display the owner's collection of artifacts that are relevant to the concept and theme of the space. The walls throughout have a skim coat of smooth stucco which, according to Jack Baum, "has been hand distressed to evoke years of benign neglect—characteristic of the places described in the novel." The 14 ft. ceiling has been left exposed to the existing structure and the ceiling has also been artfully aged. The chairs and ottomans are custom-designed "to suggest a poor man's night club in the style of the 1930s." Garment quality leather, in a natural distressed hide finish, covers the chairs. Opposite the bar is a long, traditional banquette covered in a matching leather.

Small groups can be accommodated on a small raised space with a terrazzo floor which is located at the rear of the space. This area is separated from the service station beyond by a low wall of distressed painted wood infilled with steel mullioned windows with distressed amber glass—to match the storefront's design. Simple pendant lamps, reminiscent of early lighting fixtures that may have been found in Mexico back then are combined with custom sconces adapted from hurricane style candle-holders to create the warm, intimate lighting of Under the Volcano.

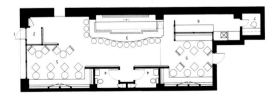

REVOLUTION

MANCHESTER, UK

Design ▪ Caulder Moore, London, UK
Designer ▪ Ian Caulder
Photography ▪ Adrian Wilson

Revolution is starting a real upheaval in the United Kingdom as it appears in unexpected and unusual settings that vary from capitalistic, deserted bank buildings to proletarian, working class garages and factories. As conceived and designed by Ian Caulder of Caulder Moore of London, "The individual design allows each location to maintain its strength, interest, individuality and character."

The one thing that all the evolutionary, Revolution-ary cafés have in common—in addition to extensive vodka bars—is "the eclectic, raw, individual energy that the design utilizes from the existing architectural structure of the building and translates the brand's energy into an aspirational interior." Wherever and whenever feasible, double height spaces are

exploited and often floor-to-ceiling features such as mirrors and the vodka vaults will stretch up from the ground floor through the voids up to the upper level. "The result is a dramatic and exciting concept that stays true to the raw and authentic origins of the brand."

In keeping with the name—and the 70 premium vodkas and 30 flavored ones—RED is the color of choice. Red appears in myriad shades, textures, and fabrics from the sumptuous, gold-fringed red velvet draperies pulled over the aged, exposed brick or wood walls or windows, to the puffy burgundy leather sofas and the sharp and startlingly bright accent pillows and stool pads. Such design "signatures" such as chandeliers, overscaled and dramatically finished fireplaces, and soft, casual seating clusters make each Revolution part of the brand, and yet unique in how these elements were adapted and used. Illustrated here are views of the flagship Revolution in Manchester along with some other the other vodka cafés in the chain.

KOST·TO·KOST

ROME, ITALY

Design ▪ Studio Ciccotti, Rome
Photography ▪ Courtesy of Studio Ciccotti

ou have to go to Rome just to get on board for an imaginary train ride through the United States. Studio Ciccotti took its inspiration for this casual dining and drinking establishment from the old American movies that are so popular with many Europeans. Starting at the "Main Station," the culinary tour makes stops in New York City, New Orleans, The Grand Canyon (with detours to the O.K. Corral and a shoot-em-up old west saloon) to San Francisco. Fitted into the large space under an exposed metal truss roof with partially exposed HVAC conduits, ducts and vents, each area is a fun and fanciful cliché of what those places really are like.

The 19th century station serves as the entrance into Kost-To-Kost and it is finished with solid wood panels, ship-lapped slats on the main room walls and plastered over in the check room. The checkroom door resembles a ticket office with a lift-up flap and a lower access door. Posters of the various "stopping off" destinations are strategically located in this area which has rustic, larch wood planked floors. Two vintage-style wood benches serve in the waiting room area where patrons waiting for a table are kept company by a mannequin dressed as an Indian—as seen in the old-time western horse operas.

The trip begins along the railway tracks that lead into the first dining area. The 75 cm steel rails are set in wood "sleepers" and pebbles are strewn in between the wood timbers. A reproduction of a locomotive that serves as the cash-desk also becomes the access control unit for the restaurant and the closed circuit TV allows the supervisor to control the action on the floor from this vantage point. The "locomotive" is fashioned out of iron plate and painted. Set in between the large structural pilasters that support the longitudinal axis of the space are wooden cubicles that suggest the train compartments. These booths are actually the main seating area and the fixed seats are upholstered in vinyl and fabrics and have stained wood sides and bases. Separating these "compartments" are dividers of laminated wood with half glass "windows" and pull close drapery. Adding to the sense of authenticity are the notices and accessories one might have found on old-time trains: luggage racks stacked with vintage satchels, and valises, stop handles, class demarcations and such.

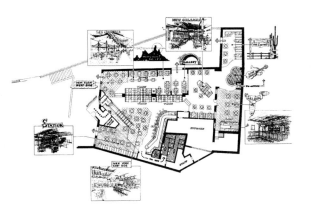

New York is the first "stop" and also the location of the main bar. Faux textured bricks, on the walls, are finished with shadows of yesteryear advertisements and signs. A stylized reproduction of the Statue of Liberty is the focal point here along with the lattice on the ceiling over the rear counter where TV monitors, signs and posters of noted tourist spots in New York City are illustrated. The Golden Gate Bridge-realized in iron plate, steel ropes and pipes and reticulated grillwork—takes over in San Francisco. The laminated woodwork with its undulating edge is meant to represent the Bay under the blue painted sky/ceiling. The floor is a resinous screed of the same watery blue color.

The Grand Canyon is affected with wall murals of the characteristic rocks and stones. The gallery—or tunnel—beyond is an arched structure clad within by precast cement that represents the rocky finish shown on the exterior arch. The American style, freestanding tables and chairs are set out beneath gray varnished, plasterboard which resembles the smoke stained tunnel roof.

New Orleans is divided into three seating zones. One has free standing tables, another has fixed seating inside a stylized Mississippi riverboat and the last zone has booths set along the right hand side. All seats and backrests are covered with striped fabrics and the chairs and tables are painted. The sky blue ceiling is somewhat reflected in the colored resin screed used on the floor. The part below the "boat" suggests the color of the river's water.

The final areas are the Far West Saloon with its horizontal strips of wood and the half doors made of louvered panels and the O.K. Corral which is all wood and has a floor painted to look like desert sand. The transformation from area to area—location to location—is fun and affords guests a great ole time in the U.S. of A. without ever needing to get their passports stamped.

GORDON BIERSCH

LAGUNA HILLS, CA

Design ▪ Allied Architecture & Design,
San Francisco, CA
Roddy Creedon/Martin Austria, Jr. /Michael Chen
Erin Lilly/John B. Lin/Kotting Luo/
Liu-Chuen Loh/Jeshua Paone/
Mark Schwettmann/Bryan Young
Photography ▪ Courtesy of Allied Architecture
& Design

Allied Architecture & Design approached the design of the Gordon Biersch Café & Brewery in Laguna Hills, CA by stripping away the interior walls and ceiling of what was an abandoned bank building located at the edge of a suburban mall parking lot. What was "revealed" was a "building with barn-like clarity; four masonry block walls spanned by heavy timber trusses, supporting a high gabled roof."

Inspired by the "hand crafting and authenticity of tradition German beer brewing," the architects/designers added rich mahogany, Douglas fir, hand wrought iron, and areas of masonry to create the desired interior which now houses a bar, a dining room and a working beer brewery. The brewery "weaves in and out of the north wall activating both the bar and dining areas, while exposing its inner workings to the street."

For the actual layout of the space, the program was organized around an exiting cruciform diagram established by arched concrete openings at the center of each of the four block walls. "A central freestanding volume of brick was inserted to define two of the three major program elements of bar and dining—while maintaining the singular nature of the existing space." Unifying it all is the warm, gentle neutral color palette

with subtle celadon green, pale gold and earth color tinted walls. These are accented by the sharp black metal moldings around the large panes of glass that separate, but make visible, the Brewery from the other areas of the café. To create more intimate dining spaces under the high pitched, wood timber beamed roof, canopies extend out over the upholstered booth seating which is set beside the brick covered walls. Lighting fixtures are recessed into the cantilevered canopies or angle out from a light bar. Uplights on the columns and wall sconces on the walls add to the warm, intimate feeling of the woodsy setting.

THIRSTY BEAR

SAN FRANCISCO, CA

Design ▪ Allied Architecture & Design,
San Francisco, CA
Roddy Creedon/Martin Austria, Jr./
Michael Chen/David Godarian/Jerry Jai/
Kotting Luo Lih-Chuin Loh/Jeshua Paone/
Mark Schwettmann / William Taylor
Photography ▪ Allied Architecture & Design

Since the two story, building, located in the South of Market district of San Francisco, has frontage on two streets, the designers architects, Allied Architecture & Design, felt that this " suggested a design approach that structured a 'see-through' building in both plan and section."

The front and rear facades were partially peeled away and replaced with a steel moment frame filled in with multi-hued panes of glass. "Different glazing characteristics are used to create varying degrees of opacity—presenting the transparency of the building through a dynamic set of filters." In the same manner, AAD peeled away the existing interior floors and connected the three levels with service volumes and stairs suspended in between. Old broken, stained and even painted areas of the original brick walls have been incorporated into the now fun and open space with the stained concrete floors and colorful painted accents of red, lime green, pumpkin orange and saffron yellow. The breakthroughs from one level to the next visually connect the various dining areas. The open kitchen with its lemon yellow soffit that soars to the upper level and the kitchens surrounded by stainless steel make it the focal point at ground level and visible from almost anyplace in the Thirsty Bear.

The informal dining is mainly at loose tables with red tops and metallic gray chairs while on the upper level, in architectural niches backed up by the brickwork and the telltale evidence of a previous existence, black vinyl banquettes are lined up. Over them hang colorful posters and artwork. "Visual privacy or connectivity between the levels is modulated via glass mosaic doors and moveable glass screens" that add accents of bright color that echo those colors already used throughout the open café.

BUTTERFLY JAZZ CLUB

SAN FRANCISCO, CA

Design ▪ Allied Architecture & Design,
San Francisco CA
Martin Austria, Jr./Roddy Creedon/John B. Lin/
Lih Chuin Loh/Kotting Luo/Jeshua Paone/
Mark Schwettmann
Photography ▪ Allied Architecture & Design

The 1920's era when Jazz flourished has been recaptured and reinvented as the setting for the Butterfly Jazz Club in San Francisco's Mission District. With Allied Architecture & Design setting the design stage, three generous openings were cut into the existing facade of a defunct auto body garage and then "interlaced with storefront and glazing of various opacity and color" to offer pedestrians, out front, a "perception of what's going on inside." This blurred boundary activates the nighttime landscape of this developing section of San Francisco.

Inside, the designers used the original, 1920's brick walls, timber trusses and wood tongue-in-grove ceiling to "define the setting for an investigation into the relevance of the rhythmic and spatial aspects of jazz music to the formal and material elements of an architectural language." To reflect the existing context of the light industrial construction, the designers found their inspiration in the Blue Note album covers of the 1950s and 1960s and thus browns, yellows and blues predominate in the color scheme. Bent wall planes, gently tapered ceiling plates and multifaceted folded glazing systems "further orchestrate the play and they are arranged to intensify their syncopated character and implied interactions."

B.B. KING/
LUCILLE'S BAR

NEW YORK, NY

Design: Morris Nathanson Design, Pawtucket, RI
Josh Nathanson/Kim Nathanson D'Oliveira
Photography: Warren Jagger

ew York City and the Disney Corporation revo-
lutionized 42nd St. and took it away from the
sex shops and tawdry businesses and have
turned in back into what is was and was always
meant to be: the heart and soul of the
Entertainment District. Now joining the illustrious
names that are flocking back to this historic street is
Danny Bensusan's B.B. King—a new adventure in dining, drinking and music.

As designed by the Morris Nathanson Design firm,
a fully illuminated neon and electric light marquee
stretches out over 42nd St. to let everyone know that
B.B. King is here. Guests enter through the street level
retail shop with the B.B. King branded merchandise
and descend into the 500-seat hall with theatrical
lighting, special acoustics and concert style seating
that faces the red velvet framed stage. The 1940s style
room with its dark, custom carpeted floor and mix-
ture of loose furniture, booths and banquettes "complement the musical experience." Especially nice
touches are the old "vinyl" records set into the top of
each blue table top; the black vinyl, high-backed
booths along the faux brick wall, the pull back red
draperies between the booths and the painting/assem-
blage/collage artwork of Mark Tabor. The angled mirror border allows for better viewing of the stage and
the vertical wall light fixtures suggest the bye-gone
time—the same time that inspired the art deco pattern of the carpeting.

Guests can also visit Lucille's Bar, shown here,
which is a more intimate area for dining or a bar visit
before or after the performance. As designed by Josh
Nathanson and Kim D'Oliveira, the front of the bar is
tufted red leather with a zinc top and the dark wood
of the back bar creates a spectacular presence in the
low illumination space. A tribute to B.B. King's gui-
tar—Lucille—is center stage on the back bar.

Corrugated frosted glass panels, set in mahogany
stained dividers add a nostalgic touch to the space.
The seating combines loose, booth and banquette
seating on the mostly red, swirl-patterned carpet. The
black vinyl upholstery is piped in white and the nail-
headed trimmed banquettes are covered in alternating
bands of black and white. Rich, cherry wood colored
paneling covers the wall and an opening in the ceiling
visually connects Lucille's with the entrance level.

BLUE NOTE

LAS VEGAS, NV

Design: Morris Nathanson Design, Pawtucket, RI
Tom Limone/Kim N. D'Oliveira
Photography: Warren Jagger

"The Blue Note is synonymous with cool, classy, soulful music and we're happy to bring that tradition to Las Vegas," said Danny Bensusan, the owner of the famous Blue Note CafÈ in New York City which is "a celebrated and acclaimed musical treasure and an institution of American culture." To get it just right for the 17,000 sq. ft. space in the Desert Passage at the Aladdin Hotel/ Casino in Las Vegas, Morris Nathanson Design was commissioned to create the interior which combines a 500-seat club with stage and a 150 seat café. The former is probably the only "upscale concert venue in Las Vegas" while the more intimate café is dominated by a giant video screen that showcases Jazz greats and their performances.

Blue is the color that permeates and completely engulfs the tiered club/theater with its full stage framed with blue velvet drapes that match the dark painted walls, the laminated tabletops and the upholstered seats. Stretching across the width of the space myriad light tracks carry a full compliment of theatrical lighting fixtures. A blue and gold patterned carpet covers the different levels and the steps connecting them. At the rear of this room is a long, mahogany faced bar that is interrupted by an arcade of columns covered part way up with large, bright blue glazed ceramic tiles. The continuous sweep of the blue painted arches frame the bar and accentuate the heroic scaled, mahogany and glass shelved back bar. Uplighting, in this area, creates a lovely visual glow that while not detracting from the music club lighting

does point up the bar. On the floor there are swirling patterns of dark green, sienna red, mustard gold and off white vinyl flooring materials.

In the café, horizontal banded piers covered with mahogany and cherry woods break up the larger areas of creamy colored walls. The walls are almost completely covered with framed pictures of Jazz artists and Blues greats. Red velvet draperies and a giant white ceiling ring in an otherwise black ceiling delineates this more informal performance area. Track lighting and recessed high hats light up the "stage" while lighting set over the angled-for-viewing mirror panels, that create a border over the row of booths lined up along the perimeter wall, illuminate the pictures on the wall. Dubonnet and black leather are used to cover the booth seating and the loose seating set out on the light, natural wood floor. Thanks to the tilted mirrors, diners seated in the booth can look up and see reflected the action on the performance stage.

This area has its own mahogany-faced bar and an octagonal shaped column, sheathed in the two colors of wood, pierces the second white ceiling circle which serves to highlight the bar's location. "The intimate bar, the dark mellow colors and the many framed pictures allow the guests to immerse themselves in the music and romance of the Jazz experience."

INDEX BY DESIGN FIRM